ESSAYS ON THE RITUAL
OF SOCIAL RELATIONS

Essays on

THE RITUAL OF SOCIAL RELATIONS

by

DARYLL FORDE
MEYER FORTES
MAX GLUCKMAN
VICTOR W. TURNER

edited by

MAX GLUCKMAN

MANCHESTER
UNIVERSITY PRESS

© 1962 MANCHESTER UNIVERSITY PRESS

Published by the University of Manchester at
THE UNIVERSITY PRESS
316–324, Oxford Road, Manchester 13

Distributed in the U.S.A. by
HUMANITIES PRESS, INC.
303, Park Avenue South, New York 10, N.Y.

First published 1962
Reprinted 1966

TO THE MEMORY

OF

ARNOLD VAN GENNEP

Printed in Great Britain by Butler & Tanner Ltd., Frome and London

PREFACE

In 1959 Dr. Emrys Peters, then in charge of the Department of Social Anthropology in the University of Manchester, succeeded in persuading Professors E. E. Evans-Pritchard, C. D. Forde, and M. Fortes to deliver three lectures in 1960 under the Simon Fund (Social Sciences), and he arranged for the publication of the lectures by the University Press. Since Professor Evans-Pritchard lectured on quite a different topic, 'Anthropology and History', the Press decided it would be best to publish his lecture separately. Two lectures on their own do not make a book, so Dr. Peters asked our visitors if they would agree to the inclusion of an essay by Dr. Turner of our own Department (who had at one time held a Simon Fellowship), and a covering essay by myself. They generously agreed to this, even though this meant a year's delay in publication, and though it meant that their own essays, prepared for delivery to a general audience including undergraduate students of anthropology and 'laymen', would appear alongside essays prepared for delivery to an advanced seminar of staff and postgraduate students.

The origin of this book thus lies in our ability under the Simon Fund to invite distinguished colleagues to lecture in the University. I therefore take this opportunity of acknowledging how much that Fund has assisted the development of our Department, since its foundation in 1949. By enabling us to invite Visiting Professors and Research Fellows of senior as well as junior status, the Fund has enabled us to learn directly of work elsewhere, and to maintain continuity in our own research. The occasional lectures it has financed, like the two published here, have added immensely to the stimulus our colleagues from elsewhere were able to give us. I record these facts in gratitude to the late Lord Simon of

Wythenshawe. When he established the Simon Fund for the University, there was no Department of Social Anthropology in the University, and I am sure he did not have the study of tribal society in mind when he endowed the social sciences. But as soon as he realized that anthropologists dealt with general problems of social life, his lively interest in all things human was awakened and characteristically he followed the development of our work with great sympathy. We owe much to him in many ways.

MAX GLUCKMAN

University of Manchester,
September 1961

CONTENTS

CONTENTS

LES RITES DE PASSAGE[1]

by MAX GLUCKMAN

THE four essays in this book deal with ceremonies which were characterized as 'Rites de Passage' by Arnold van Gennep, in his book published under that title in 1909. In my essay I set out his main theory, which was about the sequence of rites used to alter people's social relationships. I then set out Van Gennep's statements on the nature of the social relationships within which the rites were set, and suggest that though these statements were often very illuminating and penetrating, they were disconnected from one another. I argue that because he lacked an adequate theory about the nature of society he was unable to develop implications which he himself sensed in his major, very important, discovery. This may have been because he felt that, in order to validate this discovery, he had to prove that rites de passage occurred very widely through many societies and in many situations in each society, since this was the mode of proof current among the kind of anthropologists on whose work he was commenting, and whose ideas he was criticizing and trying to develop. It seems that in this way he was blocked from proceeding to a deeper analysis, so that his book now may appear on the whole rather boring to a modern social anthropologist. Nevertheless I emphasize the tremendous contribution he made, and the extent to which he stimulated

[1] I am grateful to the Ford Foundation for a grant for my personal research, which has eased my task in doing the research for this essay, as for other work. Professor Ely Devons and my wife assisted me greatly by their comments on the essay itself, as I wrote it; and for later help I am deeply indebted to Professors Forde and Fortes, to Dr. Martin Southwold, and to my colleagues in various fields at Manchester, particularly to Drs. E. Peters and V. W. Turner.

I

and improved the recording of tribal rituals. I proceed then to discuss the change in the modes by which social anthropologists now analyse rituals, as against the modes of analysis of our predecessors like Van Gennep and Sir James Frazer; and I try to produce a general proposition to explain one problem set by Van Gennep: why is it that in tribal society there is on the whole greater ritualization of transitions in social status, and greater ritualization indeed of social relationships in general, than there is in modern society?

Van Gennep's *Les Rites de Passage* was one of the most important books written about ritual in the generation before the First World War, and his 'discovery' was to make a greater impression on subsequent work than books which are much better known, at least outside France, like Tylor's *Primitive Culture*, Frazer's *The Golden Bough*, and Marett's *The Threshold of Religion*.

The value of his analysis, and the depth of some of his almost casual asides,[1] concealed on occasion in footnotes, are emphasized explicitly in Professor Fortes's essay; the value of his main pioneering discovery is acknowledged by Professor Forde and Dr. Turner. He argued that rituals dealing with movements of people and groups on the land and of persons between groups, and with movements into new statuses, such as in pregnancy and childbirth, at initiation, at betrothals and marriage, and at funerals, as well as rituals at changes of the seasons and phases of the moon, at sowing and first fruits and harvest, at ordinations and installations, exhibited a common order. There was first a 'separation' from the old state of things or previous social condition, then a 'marginal' period, and then an 'aggregation' to a new condition, or 'reaggregation' to the old—phases which Van Gennep's translators describe as rites of separation, rites of

[1] See the references in S. T. Kimball's 'Introduction' to the recent translation by Vizedom and Caffee (1960), at pp. ix–xii.

2

transition, and rites of incorporation. He stated that changes in social relations involving movements between groups, or alterations of status, in semi-civilized societies with their conceptions of magico-religious bases for groups, disturbed both the life of society and the life of the individual, and the function of *rites de passage* was to reduce the harmful effects of these disturbances. Since so many of the rites aimed at the same purpose, they naturally took on a similar form, and this appeared most dramatically in the recurrence of rites, among important ceremonies of different peoples, in which death in one condition was enacted, and resurrection into another condition. Van Gennep stressed that in different situations various of these three stages might be emphasized: thus rites of separation are prominent in funerals, while rites of incorporation are marked in weddings, and rites of transition at initiation ceremonies. The phase of transition sometimes develops an autonomy of its own, and becomes a 'liminal' (threshold) period between two more firmly established states. This liminal period tends to be 'sacred', for he saw social life in early civilizations as constant movement between 'the sacred world' and 'the profane world'.[1]

Van Gennep began his analysis by using 'territorial passages' for his framework, and he examined how when persons moved across borders, or entered at thresholds of houses and temples, they observed rituals. These rites of crossing the threshold gave him an alternative terminology of preliminal, liminal, and postliminal rites. In modern parlance, he used these territorial passages to establish his model for all *rites de passage*. But his main treatment was of rites at the so-called 'life-crises': birth, initiation, marriage, and death. Many anthropologists have used the phrase, *rites de passage*, as a distinguishing category for these rituals, on the whole reserving 'initiation' for rituals at 'adolescence', though

[1] *Op. cit.*, Ch. I.

Van Gennep considered under that head also entry into priesthoods and even into occupations. The taking over of Van Gennep's phrase is in itself a tribute to the insight which enabled him to perceive how widespread was this particular ordering of rites, an ordering which has been validated in hundreds of subsequent recordings, all enriched by the lessons taught by Van Gennep. Indeed, some anthropologists had probably not consulted his original analysis when they paid tribute to him by using his schema. His categorization of seasonal and agricultural rituals, as *rites de passage*, crammed into a final chapter, received less attention; but his schema also enriched observation and analysis of these rites.

I must add that Van Gennep did not of course believe that the *passage* explained the whole of a ceremony: each ceremony, he pointed out, had specific protective, propitiatory, acquisitive, purificatory, productive, and/or predictive purposes, according to its situation in social life.

I think that the main impact of Van Gennep's thesis was on the study of the mechanism of rituals, rather than on the role which whole ceremonies and specific rites play in the ordering and re-ordering of social relations. Van Gennep clearly had this background to the rites in mind when he worked out the mechanism of *rites de passage*. Thus, as Fortes points out, he insisted that even where membership of a caste or social class is hereditary, the child is not a 'complete' member by birth alone: on the contrary, a child must be incorporated into its group by ceremonies in which the politico-legal and social aspect is more marked than the magico-religious.[1] Again, he distinguished between social and physical return to ordinary life of a mother after child-birth, between social marriage and sexual union, between

[1] French ed., p. 143; trans., p. 101.

4

social and physical puberty, and between social and physical parenthood.[1] He also saw birth ceremonies as separating the baby from the asexual world, the world preceding human society, and as containing rites to incorporate the child into the society of the sexes and into the nuclear or extended family and other groups.[2] He emphasized that tribal societies consist of a variety of sub-groups, movements between which involve rites akin to baptism and ordination;[3] and above all he stressed that while modern societies reduce as far as they can the distinction between male and female, this distinction plays a far more important role among semi-civilized peoples, who rigidly separate men and women in economic, political, and especially magico-religious activities.[4] (It is worth noting that Durkheim, in his *De la division du travail social*, argued—incorrectly—the opposite, though it is true that he had written his book some fifteen years before Van Gennep who had better data to consult.) Indeed, Van Gennep in a footnote[5] suggested that the purpose of clitoridectomy may be to remove 'the appendage by which the female resembles the male', but he did not correspondingly suggest that circumcision removes that part of the male organ which resembles the vulva: he treated circumcision as a mere operation on a conveniently separable part of the body, like paring of nails or extracting teeth.[6] Again, as Fortes says in his essay, Van Gennep saw that initiation rites confer social puberty by incorporating boys and girls into the adult society of sexes. From now on they are ready for marriage, which is quite different from sexual relations:[7] incidentally, he saw a clear distinction

[1] French ed., p. 65; trans., p. 46.
[2] French ed., p. 74; trans., p. 52.
[3] French ed., p. 2; trans., p. 2.   [4] *loc. cit.*
[5] French ed., p. 104; trans., p. 72.
[6] French ed., p. 109, n.1; trans., p. 75.
[7] French ed., pp. 97–8; trans., p. 67.

between sexual relations as such and marriage in breach of exogamy.[1]

In a different realm of relations, Kimball says in his 'Introduction' to the translation (at p. x) that Van Gennep anticipated Malinowski's analysis of reciprocity: but in practice Van Gennep only threw in a statement that the duty of royalty among the 'semi-civilized' to re-distribute the gifts they received, creates a continuous social bond like a communion, as a parallel to exchange of gifts on ceremonial occasions. He later elaborates this into a 'theory' of the 'centralization and decentralization' of wealth to avoid 'concentration'; but he does this in one sentence ending a very pertinent footnote on the function of marriage-payments for a bride.[2]

Van Gennep also has some penetrating interpretations of rites themselves, as reflecting the structure of social relations and changes in these relations. Thus in discussing the 'capture' of a bride among Arabs, and the reluctance to leave her home which the bride must show, he details how in the rites she is separated from the girls of her own age-group; and he says that if the ritual were a survival of rape, the whole of the girl's people would resist her abduction.[3] As it is, only two age-groups are involved in the simulated struggle: for these rites express the resistance of the group which is losing a member.[4] If we remember when he wrote,

[1] French ed., p. 190; trans., p. 133.

[2] French ed., pp. 43 and 171; trans., pp. 31 and 120.

[3] French ed., p. 178; trans., p. 125.

[4] Dr. Emrys Peters points out to me that there are hidden difficulties in this interpretation, since marriage may be to a parallel first cousin. He suggests that the custom of 'capture' is related to the separation of male and female roles: the bride is 'captured' with the connivance of her father and taken to his tent; she resists males and injures them, and is applauded for this by the women. Peters adds that Robertson Smith dealt better with the point, which Van Gennep takes from Burkhardt on the Sinai Bedouin.

we must admire how clearly he saw this 'marriage by capture' as ritual arising out of present–day relations.[1] Again, he saw clearly that 'sacredness' is not absolute but relative to the situation. Brahmans are always sacred, but there is a hierarchy of Brahman families, some of which are more sacred than others. A woman (apparently everywhere) is congenitally impure, but sacred in relation to all adult men when pregnant, and to most other women.[2] This was a theme of shifting sacredness and profaneness which Srinivas was to develop far in his analysis of *madi* (purity) and *pole* (pollution) among the Coorgs of S. India.[3] Van Gennep saw too that performing in public for the first time the tasks of a new status symbolized the assumption[4] of new ranges of responsibility: Fortes praises him for this vision.

I have tried to list almost all Van Gennep's statements on social relations in order to do justice to his perspicacity and achievement; but I have merely been able to list them, since I do not believe it is possible to work any consistent and systematic vision of social relations out of his book.[5] If this listing has bored my readers, I can only say that I myself was rather bored on recently re-reading his book twice, just because he has failed to relate his statements about social relations to one another, and to various types of ritual. I say that I find *Les Rites de Passage* boring now, though as a student I learnt to admire him: in those years, around 1930, we had few monographs by modern anthropologists to

[1] For a full elaboration of this theme, see A. W. Hoernlé (1925), p. 481 f.

[2] French ed., p. 16; trans., p. 12.

[3] M. N. Srinivas (1952).

[4] Well brought out by A. I. Richards in her analysis of girls' initiation among the Bemba of Northern Rhodesia (1956), especially at pp. 128, 129, 140.

[5] Equally he had no theory of psychological relations, and anthropologists interested in psychological problems might find that this handicapped his analysis. This falls outside my own province.

study, and I saw in looking at the reports of ethnographers, written before and after the publication of *Les Rites de Passage*, how Van Gennep's analysis had helped to improve descriptions. The advance was very marked to South African students, since we worked again and again through H. A. Junod's still classic study of the Tsonga (Thonga) of Mozambique, and Junod explicitly paid tribute to Van Gennep. Junod had published in 1898 an account, *Les Ba-Ronga*, of the peoples among whom he lived as a missionary. In 1913 he published a fuller monograph, *The Life of a South African Tribe*, with a second edition in 1927. By the time he wrote the second monograph, he had fifteen years' more experience and judgment behind him, of which ten years were spent with the tribe, and five years in Europe resting and preaching, but also writing, reflecting, and reading in anthropology.[1] Of the contemporary great scholars of religion he mentions in his book only Frazer, Marett, and Van Gennep, though I think the internal evidence shows that he had absorbed much of Durkheim, and I consider that his detailed analysis of types of offerings and sacrifices must have been written with Hubert and Mauss's 'Essai sur la nature et fonction sociale du sacrifice' by his side.[2] Similarly, his references to animism and other current concepts show how he had read Tylor and others. It is therefore most striking that he went out of his way to laud Van Gennep's analysis: 'A French [actually Flemish] anthropologist, Mr. A. van Gennep, published some years ago a book *Les Rites de Passage* ... which throws a great light on these mysterious customs' of initiation of boys in circumcision lodges. He then specifically describes the initiation rites of the Tsonga under the heads of separation rites, marginal rites, and

[1] H. P. Junod (n.d., *circa* 1934), *passim*.
[2] *Année sociologique*, ii (1899), pp. 29–138. Reprinted in Hubert and Mauss (1929).

aggregation rites. Junod also used this schema, sometimes implicitly, but mostly explicitly, to describe and discuss not only other Tsonga rituals but also much of Tsonga secular life. In short, he was inspired by Van Gennep's book to see Tsonga life as a series of *passages*, in the life of individual men and women, in seasonal and daily activities, and in sickness and in health. Tsonga make *passages* from status to status; moving or founding a village, and installing chief and headman, involve *passages*; to enter on agricultural activities Tsonga pass through *passages* associated with changes of the season, and also when they go hunting or fishing; to sleep is to *move* from waking, and to wake to *move* from sleeping; during illness and when sacrificing there is *movement* through separation from normal life, into a marginal period, from which re-aggregation has to take place. Thus Junod saw, through Van Gennep's insight, that Tsonga social life was a series of movements in space and in time, a series of changes of activity, and a series of transitions in status for individuals; and he brought out that in Tsonga society almost every one of these movements, changes and transitions was marked by ritual and taboos. I have heard both senior and youthful anthropologists say that all Van Gennep demonstrated was that everything has a beginning, a middle, and an end. Even if this were all, every important truth seems obvious once stated: I think that the development in Junod's ethnographic skills after his reading of Van Gennep, of itself proves how stimulating the concept of *rites de passage* was. Van Gennep helped raise Junod's work from run-of-the-mill reporting of customs, till it ranked, and still ranks, among the great monographs. Nevertheless, I would myself still advise a student, wishing to study *rites de passage*, to go to the persisting excitement of Junod rather than to Van Gennep himself.

Van Gennep is dull to me now in the same way as Sir

James Frazer's *The Golden Bough* is dull. *The Golden Bough* undoubtedly contains for us some seminal ideas on the associations which inspire magical practices, the germs of some ideas on the connection of the political process with seasonal festivals, including beliefs in divine kingship and the use of scapegoats. Otherwise he in effect demonstrated how widely certain ideas of magic, beliefs in souls and gods, types of taboos and festivals, were distributed. For to demonstrate the validity of his analysis, Frazer wrote twelve volumes, in which he piled example after example on top of one another of rites and beliefs, drawn from all over the world, and through all ages, to show that these rites and beliefs have occurred persistently and universally among mankind. He never analysed one rite or belief to any depth, in its social or emotional background: instead he recapitulated the same ideas through volumes of highly selected illustration.[1] Van Gennep in his first chapter criticized many of his colleagues because they did not develop a rigorous classification of beliefs and rites but instead collected parallels taken out of their social contexts and their ritual sequences. He complained that they based classifications on external similarities rather than on the dynamics of the rite.[2] His scheme of *passage* was a major step forward: but in the end he too succumbed to the prevailing methods of proof, for he too seems to have felt that he had to show that the process of *rites de passage* occurred universally. Though, as I have shown, he often touches on critical problems affecting the association of *rites de passage* with social relations, he never pursued these points, but like Frazer broke into almost casually selected illustrations, taken seemingly haphazardly from continent after continent and from era after era. The argument becomes overwhelmingly

[1] See E. E. Evans-Pritchard (1933).
[2] French ed., pp. 7 f.; trans., pp. 5 f.

convincing by repetition and recapitulation: it remains at the same point, for we are shown the same stages of *passage*, variously emphasized, in different types of society. The argument does not advance through the comparison of rites of various kinds, as does Fortes's essay, which discusses rites of initiation and installation in different situations, to raise problems concerned with the vesting of the legitimate rights and duties on persons in terms of their new status. Nor does Van Gennep penetrate deeply into any one ritual situation, as Forde and Turner do, to expose the complex adjustments of certain kinds of relations, while others which are also involved do not figure in the ceremonial.

Van Gennep for me illustrates strikingly how a man can make an important discovery, and sense that he is on the way to further problems, yet be prevented from going on to exploit his discovery because he tries to prove his initial point beyond doubt in a form which his contemporaries, and probably he himself, thought convincing. I consider that current modes of proof, in the field where he was working, stultified Van Gennep and prevented him from developing his theory further. I must stress that this applied in the field where he was working, the field tackled by Frazer, Tylor, Marett, Reville, and a large number of others cited by Van Gennep himself. There was, of course, another kind of investigation of tribal societies, which concentrated on what we would now call the functional connections between different elements of social life—by men like Maine, Engels, Durkheim, and further back, De Coulanges. When we read their books, we feel that we are conversing with modern minds, and are not bored, as I (at least) am bored by Van Gennep. Unhappily Van Gennep did not model himself on these writers, but on those early writers on ritual who proceed by accumulation rather than by analysis. This was natural enough, since it was their views that he was correcting and developing: and whatever he might have achieved with a different method, what he did achieve within the limitations of his own method was magnificent enough.

In assessing Van Gennep's achievement, we must bear in mind that he could not perhaps get further than he did because he had largely to work with bare reports of ceremonies compiled by others of widely varying skills; and that even when rites were described well the reporter was not competent to analyse the social relations in which they were set. Though Van Gennep had been among tribal societies in Madagascar, he had not studied them: he barely uses Madagascar material in *Les Rites de Passage*. Junod developed Van Gennep's theory: he knew the Tsonga and their culture extremely well. I stress the deficiencies of Van Gennep's data because these highlight what he did manage to do in working out a new schema for ritual, and in feeling beyond the ritual to the social situations in which it was set. A few paragraphs persuade me that he was on the verge of a remarkable breakthrough for the period. Early on he introduces his argument by stating that every individual moves from situation to situation, from age to age, from occupation to occupation; and hence that transitions are implicit in the very fact of existence. And in his conclusion he reaffirms that the constants of social life are movements of various kinds. But the point is most strongly stated at the end of his penultimate chapter. Here he discusses a series of rites, in Greece, India and elsewhere, in which a man who has been thought dead but who has returned home and wants to be reintegrated into his former position has to pass through rites of birth, childhood, adolescence, and remarriage to his own wife. He concludes: 'Il faudrait qu'un ethnographe pût assister à une telle succession, immédiate, d'un certain nombre d'entre les cérémonies étudiées ici, en décrivît avec le plus grand soin les phases diverses. On aurait alors la meilleure preuve, et directe, que la présente systématisation n'est pas une pure construction logique, mais qu'elle répond à la fois aux faits, aux tendances sous-jacentes et aux nécessités sociales.' [1] Junod was not present at such a sequence of ceremonies: but he did see a whole series of separate rites and the improvement in his reports between 1898 and 1913, I repeat, is itself a monument to Van Gennep's insight in setting up so dynamic a model of social life, and explaining *rites de passage* by this dynamism.

In his 'Introduction' to the English translation, Kimball (at p. xii) says that Radcliffe-Brown was examining rites and myths 'to determine their meaning and function in relation to social behaviour and a theory of social and symbolic logic', when he wrote his monograph on *The Andaman Islanders*.[2] Radcliffe-Brown, he points out, worked largely with the rituals of 'life-crises', but does not mention Van Gennep, although he must have been acquainted with Van Gennep's work, and although he handles 'ceremonial sequences . . . [with] appreciation of the dynamics of the rites of passage'.[3] I suggest that Radcliffe-Brown did not

[1] French ed., pp. 2–3, 270–1, 269; trans., pp. 3, 189–90, 188.

[2] Kimball mentions also W. Lloyd Warner's much later work on the Murngin (1937).

[3] Radcliffe-Brown carried out his field study of the Andaman Islanders in 1906–8, and began to write his book in 1908–9, before Van Gennep's *Les Rites de Passage* was published. The publication of Radcliffe-Brown's book was delayed by the 1914–18 War; but he told me he was held up initially because he first wrote his monograph as a theoretical analysis of Andamanese ritual and myth—the famous Chapters V and VI—only to have it rejected by Haddon and Rivers, who insisted that he must first report with bare comments on his data, and then give his analysis separately. He further told me that he was extremely bored by the task of presenting data without analysis. Unfortunately, I did not ask him at what point he read Van Gennep and why he did not refer to Van Gennep: he may well have felt that where their analyses were similar they had arrived at these simultaneously and independently, and that

find Van Gennep particularly stimulating, because he had himself observed the ceremonial ordering of rites which was Van Gennep's main contribution: indeed, precisely the same mechanism of ordering ritual had been analysed by Hubert and Mauss in their essay on the nature and function of sacrifice, published in 1899. Because Van Gennep had no elaborated theory of society in terms of which he could develop the relation of *rites de passage* to changes of social status, his work did not bear on Radcliffe-Brown's main treatment. A later generation of social anthropologists has often referred to Van Gennep's schema, and acknowledged it by name, but like Radcliffe-Brown these anthropologists have been concerned to develop their analyses of the *'tendances sous-jacentes'* and the *'nécessités sociales'*, rather than to elaborate on the mechanism.

The same change of emphasis has affected modern treatment of other problems in the study of ritual and religion so that, just as we have absorbed Van Gennep's schema and passed on, we are no longer concerned with the kinds of ideas on which Frazer and Tylor and similar thinkers of their period concentrated. If we, in sociological anthropology, now look to the past, it is, as I have said, to Durkheim and Max Weber, to Maine and to Engels, and thinkers of that kind, rather than to Frazer and Tylor. For us, Van Gennep and Frazer and Tylor did not understand society well enough to be of use to us. This shift in ancestry is very clear if one reads recent Frazer lectures. Here the modern anthropologist is paying tribute to Frazer: yet almost invariably he gives a lecture in which he shows that the rituals, which Frazer saw as fruits of mental processes and ideas, are in fact

---

therefore he did not need to acknowledge any debt. Radcliffe-Brown penetrated more deeply into the mechanisms of *rites de passage* than Van Gennep did. [Prof. Forde tells me he has Radcliffe-Brown's copy from 1909 to 1910.]

to be understood in terms of the social relations which are involved in the rituals. In 1948, Evans-Pritchard re-analysed *The Divine Kingship of the Shilluk of the Anglo-Egyptian Sudan* to show how the alleged ritual killing of the Shilluk king, and the coronation rituals, had to be investigated through an analysis of the distribution of population in the narrow strip of the Nile Valley, the system of patrilineal lineages and the maternal links of princes, and other forms of social organization. I myself took up the same theme in my 1952 Frazer Lecture, on *Rituals of Rebellion in South-east Africa* (published 1954), where I argued that certain agricultural ceremonies had to be understood in terms of the position of women in social relations, while other agricultural ceremonies required an investigation of the distribution of people under subsistence production, of the consequent organization of the nation into provinces with delegation of power from king to princes and chiefs, struggles for power in the royal dynasty, exploitation of those struggles by subjects, and the types of simple weapons so that each leader had his private army. Schapera in 1955 considered, under the title 'The Sin of Cain', the crime of fratricide in terms of its occurrence within an agnatic group, unable to take vengeance on its own members, as against its ability to avenge wrongs committed by outsiders. Fortes's 1956 Lecture on *Oedipus and Job in West African Religion* (published 1959) traces out different strands in the complex shrines of the Tallensi and relates each of these to different configurations in the network of Tallensi social relations. In his 1957 Lecture (published 1958) Forde showed the complexity of social contexts and the diversity of common interests that gave rise to the various forms of fetishism among the Yakö, and argued that, in analysing religion and ritual and magic, attention must be paid to specific ecological environments, as well as to social relations and psychological patterns.[1] Firth's *The Fate of the Soul*, and Wilson's *Divine Kingship and 'The Breath of Men'*, similarly look at beliefs with the main emphasis on the context of social relations.

Fürer-Haimendorf's Frazer Lecture on 'The After-life in Indian Tribal Belief' is mainly on belief, but he ends by stressing the importance of the sociological approach.[2]

I do not myself consider that, because we feel we have passed the point at which Frazer's basic ideas were useful, and because we now read him for antiquarian interest and often find him dull, therefore these lectures are no longer a tribute to him. When we see, as we think, further, we are perched on his shoulders, dwarfs on a giant. Hence when I state that the essays of my colleagues here published go far beyond the point which Van Gennep reached, but they are nevertheless a tribute to his genius, and appropriately dedicated to him, it is in recognition of the fact that when the pupil outdoes the master, it is often by the master's rule. Van Gennep, as I have said in effect, was outdone by Junod; and both Junod and Van Gennep are outdone by modern analyses. But we advance in no small measure because of their work.

These three essays all make their advance in terms of the same kind of approach to *rites de passage* which has marked the Frazer Lectures I have outlined above; and I need barely do more than refer to their contents. Fortes develops the full implications of Van Gennep's perception that initiation ceremonies mark and organize 'the transition from childhood to socially recognized adulthood . . . they are the means of divesting a person of his status as a child in the domestic domain and investing him with the status of actual or potential citizen in the politico-jural domain' (as Fortes puts it). In discussing this situation, and the situation created by the installation of chiefs, Fortes is concerned with

[1] Forde (1957).   [2] p. 48.

elaborating the nature of society as a network of offices, a complex of linkages between statuses and roles; and with discerning how ritual establishes and maintains this network: 'Ritual presents office to the individual as the creation and possession of society or a part of society into which he is to be incorporated through the office. Ritual mobilizes incontrovertible authority behind the granting of official office and status and thus guarantees its legitimacy and imposes accountability for its proper exercise.'

Forde was confronted with an apparently anomalous situation among the Yakö of Nigeria. Most analyses of funeral ceremonies have dealt with 'social recognitions and readjustments . . . within kin groups following death, [but] these do not receive elaborate ritual expression or major emphasis' in Yakö mortuary ceremonial. Though relations between groups of kin are involved in the ceremonial, 'the most prominent relations of the bereaved kin, and the ceremonial and practical activities that these entail, are with external groups to which the dead man belonged and to which his kin are called upon to fulfil obligations'. These external groups are chiefly the associations, in which are vested the exercise of ritual and secular power in the community. Forde's treatment of this typical Yakö *rite de passage* is thus dominantly concerned with social relations rather than rites. We had previously known of societies like the Herero with double unilineal systems of descent: their inner dynamics were made clear only when Forde studied this form of organization among the Yakö. A complex situation is created by the division of property and powers and responsibilities between agnatic and matrilineal groups, made more complicated by the fact that different agnatic groups reside together in large villages. Social order is largely maintained by various associations; and Forde shows how the death of an elder is followed by demands from the several associations to which he belonged that his place be filled, to reconstitute the network of ties based on diverse membership of individuals—and through them of their kin-groups—in this network.

Turner is more directly concerned with the actual mechanism of the *rite de passage* of initiation among the Ndembu of Northern Rhodesia. He analyses in detail the 'meaning' of three of the main symbols used in the ceremony, by looking first at their exegesis, which is how the Ndembu themselves interpret the symbols. Second, he analyses what people and groups do around and with the symbols. Third, he relates the symbols to other symbols used in the same set of rites. Thus he deals directly with the same problem as Van Gennep: how the *passage* of boys from boyhood to social adulthood is symbolized in ritual. In addition, when examining what is done with the symbol (he calls this the operational context of the symbol) he elaborates how groups and *personae* are actually mobilized around the symbols; and this involves him in an analysis of the social groupings and relationships of Ndembu which are relevant in the context of initiation. Here he probes into the web of conflict and co-operation, to quote Simmel, which composes Ndembu society—a view of society which Van Gennep hinted at in the beginning of his work, but which he used only occasionally in his main sections.

I have summarized the themes of my colleagues' essays to show how they all, as might be expected, approach *rites de passage* from the context of social relations, and my summaries are not meant to evaluate their essays, or to begin to represent these. They are in this book, to speak for themselves. I have tried to put them in the general context of the development of social anthropology, within which I have evaluated Van Gennep's theory. Having done this, I want to put forward my own tentative answers to some of the

general problems that Van Gennep raised. At the very beginning of his book, he stated that 'A mesure qu'on descend
la série des civilisations, ce mot pris dans son sens le plus
large, on constate une plus grande prédominance du monde
sacré sur le monde profane, lequel dans les sociétés les moins
évoluées que nous connaissions englobe à peu près tout:
naître, enfanter, chasser, etc., sont alors des actes qui tiennent
par la plupart de leurs côtés au sacré. De même les sociétés
spéciales sont organisées sur des bases magico-religieuses, et
le passage de l'une à l'autre prend l'aspect du passage spécial
qui se marque chez nous par les rites déterminés, baptême,
ordination, etc. . . .' He goes on to explain how, whenever a
person moves between the groups which compose society
at this level, these acts are accompanied by ceremonies,
because to the semi-civilized mind no act is entirely free
from the sacred. He contrasts this with the modern situation
where only when a laymen becomes a priest, or a priest is
defrocked, is there this movement between sacred and profane worlds.[1]

Van Gennep was here clearly thinking of 'sacred' in a
particular way. He was surely aware that at levels of civilization far above the tribal, men believed that every one of
their actions was 'sacred', in the sense that every action had
to be assessed in relation to the schemes of God or gods, so
that men were full of piety. His context makes clear that he
was thinking of those special ceremonials which are so
characteristic of tribal societies, and the peoples of the early
city-states, ceremonials in which people performed prescribed actions according to their relationships with one another. That is, father, mother, brother, sister, mother's
brother, and other kin, spouses, men and women, aged and
young, magistrates and people, are required to act in ways
that typify their roles in relation to one another. Durkheim's

[1] French ed., pp. 2 f.; trans., pp. 1 ff. Cf. my summary of Junod, above.

discussion of the regression of religion which accompanies the developing division of labour is not as clear as his discussion of changes in law. He describes in one place how religion occupies a smaller and smaller portion of social life, so that no longer is everything social also religious. He stresses the uninterrupted decline in formalism, as gods become less particularistic and confined to particular objects, and interfere less and less in human affairs, till the situation is reached where the 'God of humanity necessarily is less concrete than the gods of the city or the clan' . . . and 'one no longer attaches great importance to simple neglect of religious practices . . .' [1] Durkheim is clearly correct if he here intended also to cover the change from a situation in which social relationships, in detail, are ritualized, as against the situation in which congregations assemble to worship a general God, and each man is in communion with the Deity. It is to the former situation that I want to apply the term 'ritualization' as against the 'ritualism' of, say, the Catholic service when it is contrasted with the Protestant service.[2]

I am here entering on grounds of acute and learned dispute and disputation among students of comparative religion. In a recent article Goody has set out some of the disputation which has accumulated and enlightened—and perhaps confounded—the study of 'Religion and Ritual: the Definitional Problem'.[3] The complexity of his argument, as well as the mass of his learned citations, justify me in avoiding, dur-

---

[1] E. Durkheim (1893), pp. 138 f., 267 f.; trans. by G. Simpson (1933), pp. 169 f., 283 f.

[2] Dr. V. Turner has commented on this passage, that certain Protestant theologians attacked 'ritualism' sustainedly; and that Puritanism affected not only religious worship, but also reduced 'ceremonial' to a minimum in many other fields of activity, including drama, which they hated as 'mummery'. Their Act making stage performances illegal cut twenty odd years from Ben Jonson's playwriting.

[3] In *The British Journal of Sociology* (June 1961), pp. 142–64.

ing the course of an essay on another problem, the difficulties which are, as he shows, involved in these various definitions. I begin by stating that I consider that we cannot make pertinent distinctions and categories in this field if we try to work with too few terms, a case I have argued with respect to terminology for the study of 'law' on two occasions.[1] Goody, after examining carefully the various definitions put forward by many other scholars, as well as their substantial contributions, tries to cover all the phenomena involved in the field with virtually four terms—ritual and ceremonial, religion and magic. I respectfully suggest that if we are to avoid unnecessary and therefore obscuring terminological dispute, we must draw on the wealth of English (or whatever other language we work in) to make distinctions and categories appropriate to the problem we are tackling. Goody emphasizes this point in effect when he moves to advance his own definition of ritual as a 'category of standardized behaviour [custom] in which the relationship between the means and the end is not "intrinsic", i.e. is either irrational or non-rational'. He argues that magical action and religious acts both fall within this definition, though they are distinguishable by other criteria.[2] He moves to this point after considering Monica Wilson's distinction between ritual as 'a primarily religious action . . . directed to secure the blessing of some mystical power. . . . Symbols and concepts are employed in rituals but are subordinated to practical ends', and ceremonial as an 'elaborate conventional form for the expression of feeling, not confined to religious occasions'.[3] 'Ceremonial' is thus made a category embracing 'ritual'; as Goody says, 'For while ceremonials such as Corpus Christi Day processions which celebrate

[1] Gluckman (1955a) and (1961).
[2] Goody, *op. cit.*, especially p. 159, but also pp. 147, 157.
[3] M. Wilson (1957), p. 9.

mystical powers may perform similar functions to those like the anniversary of the October Revolution which have an exclusively secular significance, it is often useful to distinguish between them, particularly when considering the beliefs involved.' He himself concludes, as against Wilson, however, that it is simpler to apply 'ritual' to all categories of action which Wilson calls 'conventional', and to specialize 'religious' to cover activities addressed to 'some mystical power'.

Goody may well be right: this is after all an argument of convenience in which we must try to use words in the most fruitful way. I myself believe that we need to specialize 'religious' to cover actions and beliefs addressed to spiritual beings or some ultimate view of destiny, as in Buddhism; and personally I would incline to follow Wilson. That is, I would use 'ceremony' to cover any complex organization of human activity which is not specifically technical or recreational and which involves the use of modes of behaviour which are expressive of social relationships. All such modes of behaviour, conventional and stylized, are ceremonial. I would then distinguish within the field of 'ceremonial' between two separate categories, which shade into one another: the one I would call 'ceremonious' and the other 'ritual', following here Evans-Pritchard's view of magic, that 'ritual' is distinguished by the fact that it is referred to 'mystical notions', which are 'patterns of thought that attribute to phenomena supra-sensible qualities which, or part of which, are not derived from observation or cannot be logically inferred from it, and which they do not possess'.[1] If these notions are not present in the October Revolution parade, it is 'ceremonious' and not 'ritual', while the Corpus Christi Day procession is 'ritual' and not 'ceremonious' if its performance is referred to mystical

[1] Evans-Pritchard (1937), p. 12.

notions. Since both clearly have some of the same functions, we can discuss these under the more general rubric of 'ceremonial'.

Let me assure my readers that I regard my suggestions as proposals for convenience only; and I should be quite happy to have others suggested. Correspondingly, I hope that objectors to my own suggestions will not, because they object to my terminological proposals, therefore fail to scrutinize my analysis in its own right. The same plea attaches to a further specialization of terms I now suggest. As far back as 1936, I found it necessary in a thesis on 'The Realm of the Supernatural among the South-Eastern Bantu'[1] to distinguish between four kinds of 'ritual'. These were magical action, connected with the use of substances acting by mystical powers in Evans-Pritchard's sense; religious action, the cult of the ancestors, also acting in this way; substantive or constitutive ritual,[2] which expressed or altered social relationships by reference to mystical notions, and of which *rites de passage* were typical; and factitive ritual which increased the productivity or strength, or purified or protected, or in other ways increased the material well-being of a group. Factitive ritual differed from constitutive ritual in that it had more than the expression or alteration of social relationships as its end, but it embodied in it not only sacrifice to the ancestors and the use of magical substances, but also the performance of prescribed actions by members of the congregation in terms of their secular roles. Here it shaded into constitutive ritual, which consisted of such actions without the outside material end being stated; while both in turn shaded into South-Eastern Bantu

[1] D.Phil. thesis, Oxford, 1936.

[2] I first used the adjective 'substantive', but I amended this to 'constitutive' when I found that Fortes had used this better word in trying to handle the same problem. I make this acknowledgment, because I do not know that Fortes has used the word in print.

religion, in which sacrifice was the crucial rite; and obviously in sacrifice among these Bantu there is the appearance of persons by their respective roles, and they consume the sacrifice according to their relationships.

I have cited this set of distinctions partly to stress how important it may be to multiply our analytic concepts, to avoid useless disputation and to advance analysis, and partly in the incidental hope that this kind of terminology may be useful to others since I did not publish it. For my present purposes I need not adopt it. I am here, like Van Gennep, considering what I then called constitutive and factitive rituals; and I need to specialize only one term to distinguish the tendency in tribal society to make ritual use of social roles and relationships themselves in expressing and altering these, and in achieving the material prosperity of the society. I propose to use the phrase 'ritualization of social relationships'—and for brevity 'ritualization'—to define this tendency, while suggesting that 'ritualism' be reserved for those ceremonial actions in the wider religions, like Catholicism, which have highly stylized actions referable to mystical notions, but which do not develop the 'ritualism' out of the roles and relationships of the whole congregation involved. I may say that I realize that 'ritualization' might well require to be used for other purposes; but unhappily, despite diligent search, I have not been able to find another term to suit my purposes. I can only plead that my readers should from here on take 'ritualization' as referring to a stylized ceremonial in which persons related in various ways to the central actors, as well as these themselves, perform prescribed actions according to their secular roles; and that it is believed by the participants that these prescribed actions express and amend social relationships so as to secure general blessing, purification, protection, and prosperity for the persons involved in some mystical manner which is out of sensory control. For my present problems, I do not need to consider here the fine differences which may arise between the outside observer's and the participants' judgments on these actions; but by this neglect I do not mean to deny the difficulties involved here, difficulties which Goody considers thoroughly in his article.

In this sense, I believe that Van Gennep, Durkheim, and others stated a true difference between tribal and modern society when they said that there was more ritualization of social relationships in tribal society. This ritualization spreads into more specifically religious activities, as in the Bantu sacrifice, or the ceremonies of ancient Greek or of Hindu worship of gods, since these ceremonies are often performed in congregations akin in composition to the congregations of tribal society. I consider that therefore the study of modern religion raises some very different problems from the study of tribal religion and ritual, though there is a common central field. Furthermore, Durkheim was right in asserting that if one follows the development of rituals through from tribal stages to the modern industrialized stage, there is first a decline, and then a drop, in the ritualization of social relations, however much these are infused with piety. I consider that this ritualization occurs, for reasons I shall examine below, wherever people live in largish groups of kin, as they still did in Homeric Greece, in early Rome, in early Judaea, and perhaps in early Egypt, among Incas and Aztecs, and it seems to me that we still find this ritualization where this sort of situation occurs in India and China. Ritualization was apparently present in Anglo-Saxon and Viking lands, and pagan times generally, in Europe: it appears to wane with the coming of feudalism, though here we have to take into account the spread of Christianity. But Van Gennep's own citations on the Sabians, and on other Christianized peoples, indicate that there are situations in which these retain the high ritualization of specific social relationships.[1]

Van Gennep took this high ritualization of tribal societies as a datum, in the way that was customary on the whole among anthropologists of his period, instead of regarding it as setting a problem that required analysis. References such as his to the fact that among 'semi-civilized' peoples acts of transition are enveloped in ceremonies, because to the semi-civilized mind no act is entirely free from the sacred, explain little. Durkheim postulated, as others have, that this envelopment in the religious was connected with a low division of labour, though, indeed, he did not point out that religious and magical beliefs often enforced an arbitrary division of labour—as between men and women. But he merely made statements on religious development, since he said that to treat it adequately would require as much analysis as he had devoted to legal development; and he did not follow up this particular clue in his later (1913) analysis of the elements of religious life.[2] I am going to suggest that we may seek to explain this high ritualization of tribal society from the fact that each social relation in a sub-sistence economy tends to serve manifold purposes.[3] It is what I have called 'multiplex',[4] and Talcott Parsons 'diffuse'. The characteristic productive sub-groups of these societies are villages and homesteads, and also kin-groups, parts of which form the cores of residential units. The relationships between the members of these groups serve a multiplicity of purposes: they are the main productive relationships and also

[1] French ed., p. 114, on baptism among Sabians, pp. 151-2, on their initiation of priests and deacons, p. 220 (n. 3), on their funerals; English trans., pp. 79-80, 107, and 153 (n. 9) respectively.

[2] Durkheim (1913), trans. by G. W. Swain (1915).

[3] The following compressed summary is set out at somewhat greater length in Gluckman (1955b), *passim*; see also Forde (1954), 'Introduction'.

[4] See Gluckman (1955a), p. 156 *et passim*.

the relationships within which goods are mainly exchanged and consumed. Their members hold land and other property, not all in common, but subject to claims by one another. Children are reared and educated almost entirely within these groups. The groups form political units of the larger society. Finally, they may be congregations worshipping common gods together. In short, a man plays most of his roles, as several kinds of productive worker, as consumer, as teacher and pupil, as worshipper, in close association with the people whom he calls father and son and brother, wife and sister; and he shares citizenship with them, that mediated citizenship which is so marked a feature of tribal constitutional law. Moreover, all these roles are played on the same comparatively small stage, of the village and its environs, where shrines are placed about the huts or in the cattle corral, where the baby is born and the dead are buried, where the year's provender is stored. Leaving the problem of ritualization aside for the moment, it is from this situation that I see emerging the relatively great development of special customs and stylized etiquette to mark the different roles which a man or woman is playing at any one moment. That is, instead of the rather vague patterns of respect and subordination between parents and children or egalitarianism between siblings, which mark relations in our own families, we have special observances and avoidances in tribal society to denote whether a man is interacting with another as father or as son, or as uncle or nephew, brother, or grandparent or grandchild. There is even that exaggerated emphasis on differences between the sexes, to denote clearly their distinction, to which Van Gennep drew attention. In dealing with the legal aspects of tribal life, I have described Barotse relationships as 'full of custom', and argued that departures from custom are highly significant for judicial decision since they indicate breaches in fulfilling the duties of particular roles.[1] I suggest that the effect of this relatively 'exaggerated' development of custom is to mark off and segregate roles in social groups where they may be confounded.

This is, of course, not the only effect of these customs: avoidance of certain subjects in conversation with a father builds respect for the father, as do bans on the son crossing his shadow, and similar rules. This effect is more marked in the elaborate etiquette which surrounds a ruler. But, even there, we must allow for the fact that, in relatively small political units, the chief is living at the same standard as his subjects, joining with them in conversation and discussion, involved in marriage with their kin: and his specific role as ruler needs to be demarcated. Special observances mark his entry on his role as tribal priest, as against his role as tribal leader or judge. Similarly, since the head of a kinship group or village is also often priest of its congregation, he observes special customs when he takes on that role.

Junod's exploitation of Van Gennep's thesis emphasizes how important this demarcation, or segregation, of roles by special customs can be. In effect, Junod showed that almost every time that a Tsonga changed his role he underwent special practices and taboos, and special taboos and practices applied to his relatives, to mark and protect his role: when he started or ended farming, when he went fishing or hunting, when he went to war. A fortiori, this applied to situations when a Tsonga underwent a change in status.

Because men and women in tribal society play so many of their varied purposive roles with the same set of fellows, each action in addition is charged with high moral import. A man's actions as worker are not segregated from his actions as a father by being placed in a different building with a specialized set of fellows. His achievement as a farmer directly affects his position as father, as brother, as son, as

[1] *Loc. cit.*, p. 19.

husband, as priest or worshipper. That is, the moral judgment on a man who neglects his work as a cultivator applies to his relations with his wife, his children, his brothers, his chief, his subsistence group as a whole. Conversely, if a man quarrels with his wife or his brother this may affect their ability to co-operate in farming. Every activity is charged with complex moral evaluations, and default strikes not at isolated roles but at the integral relations which contain many roles. I think that it is this compound of moral evaluation, and the spreading effects of breach of role, which accounts for the way in which various roles are ritualized, and why rituals are attached to so many changes of activity, in tribal society. When a Tsonga man, who is normally a cultivator, goes hunting or fishing, he changes his role and affects his whole social milieu: and his new role is segregated by *passage* rites and by taboos, to be observed by his family and himself, from the intrusion of his other roles. Where roles are secularly segregated, moral judgments are also segregated from one another; and they do not involve that set of 'mystical' associations which characterize life in tribal societies.[1]

The social order is so impregnated with moral judgments that it can be disturbed by any failure to fulfil an obligation. This disturbance spreads and affects the group's relations with the natural world on which it is so dependent. Conversely, any disturbance of the natural world, in the form of such misfortunes as drought, crop-failure, illness, or accident, may be ascribed to disturbances of the moral and social order, represented in such beliefs as the wrath of the gods or ancestors, or the evil machinations of witches and sorcerers.

[1] I use 'mystical' as stated above in the sense that Evans-Pritchard did, *op. cit.* (1937), p. 12. 'Mystical' beliefs deal with the suprasensible, mystical operations out of sensory control. He contrasts 'mystical' with 'empirical', under sensory control.

Hence in tribal society, unlike modern society, even to harbour vicious thoughts or feelings may provoke a disturbance which brings misfortune down on one's fellows.[1] The situation may even involve beliefs that any change at all in present social arrangements is believed to provoke so great a disturbance that ritual must be performed prophylactically to redress its effects. Fortes describes in his present essay a ritual of this kind to protect the Tallensi when they are transferring land on loan. Even among those widely shifting ashbed cultivators, the Bemba, when a man cuts a new garden out of the woodland he is magically attached to it, so that he cannot lend it in the first year.[2] This system of beliefs is very highly developed among Indonesians, under the beliefs of the *adat* law.[3]

I thus see *rites de passage* as a special development of how custom and ceremonial segregate the roles of people living in the small groups of tribal society, and indeed demarcate the special purposes to which land, or huts, or stock, or material objects, are put at any one moment. I am here differentiating, as stated above, within the general field of 'ceremonial', 'ritual' from the 'ceremonious', by taking 'ritual' to be actions which are often similar to ceremonious actions, but which contain in addition 'mystical notions'. This was how Evans-Pritchard, as cited above, distinguished magical from empirical action. Ritual, that is to say, is associated with notions that its performance in some mysterious way, by processes out of sensory control, affects the well-being of the participants: it is believed to protect them or in other ways achieve their well-being. The Zulu see clearly that obeisance and other actions of respect to the

[1] See my Presidential Address to the Sociology Section of the British Association for the Advancement of Science (1961), pp. 1 f.

[2] Richards (1939), p. 185.

[3] B. Ter Haar (1948).

chief enhance his prestige: but they also believe that when he danced before his abased subjects in the first-fruits rites the prosperity and success of the nation were guaranteed.

I must at once deal with one other important factor that contributes to the relatively large number of rituals of tribal societies: their low level of technological development. In his Frazer Lecture on the manner in which 'The Context of Belief' affects approaches to fetishes among the Yakö, Forde[1] has emphasized the importance of taking account of 'the powerful drives of desire and anxiety to which [religious and magical] beliefs were everywhere harnessed' (at p. 3). He expresses disquiet at the tendency to interpret rituals in social structural or psychological terms only, and praises Malinowski's stress on 'the concern of the individual with reference to hazardous enterprises and the fear of death in the evocation and persistence of beliefs in supernatural sources both of danger and of aid' (p. 7). Forde argues cogently that beliefs and rites 'are by no means always evoked by concern for a particular social pattern, but may be stimulated by other conditions of the human environment through the values and hazards attached to material resources and techniques, the incidence of disease and other risks to health and life. . . . While beliefs and cults focused on material needs and physical well-being may be associated with or lead to the further development of patterns of social organization, such as priesthoods or institutions deriving from the prestige of a sacred chiefship, it is important to recognize that it is the ecological factors, stemming from biological and physical conditions, and the character of particular techniques, that have called them into being and sustain their significance' (pp. 7–8). Clearly, Forde is correct: rituals of all kinds are associated with efforts to ensure success and avoid disaster, and lack of success and imminence of disaster are, apparently

[1] *Op. cit., passim.*

31

at least, more openly present among tribal societies with their exiguous technology than among ourselves. Yet we are still left with the problem, why and how have tribal societies in approaching this situation worked their roles and relationships into the rituals? Why is there not a mere multiplication of individual or group magical rites, or a mere assembling of neighbourhoods in congregations pleading with the deity? And disasters—war, unemployment, strikes, lockouts, flood and drought, economic stagnation— threaten us as I write, and we cannot apparently control them, yet we do not evolve rituals of social relations to deal with our drives and anxieties.

I agree that the margin between success and disaster in tribal society contributes to the high incidence of rituals, but I am here concerned not so much with this as with the fact that social relations are so highly ritualized. *Rites de passage* have a moral, and not only a technical, component. I have tried to describe the situation in which this has to be seen. Forde sees it similarly. 'Thus the blessings sought from the *ase* [fetishes] were comprehensive and diverse. They included on the one hand the beneficent working of what we should regard as the forces of nature to maintain and protect the population. Others were social—peaceful and benevolent conduct on the part of individuals and groups and the punishment of those infringing this, whether physically or supernaturally. In public ceremonies certain associations and special cults in the village were blessed on the implied condition that they would act for its welfare.' The invocation to the *ase* personalized 'a synthetic conception of a favourable total environment, both material and social'. Concern for the security of the yam harvest, the fertility of women and the survival of children, fires and brawls, were matched by another concern, for 'the social stability of the village', which also in fact was often threatened. 'In this context, the effect of belief in the power of the *ase* was . . . both to indoctrinate, and to give confidence in, respect for moral rules.' Forde makes this kind of point continually, and he expresses my own point most cogently when he writes that 'the apprehension of the village as a total social entity was not symbolically distinguished from the non-human resources and biological processes affecting human well-being' (*loc. cit.*, pp. 10 f.).

Thus, accepting Forde's point, which has also been made to me in the discussion on this essay at Manchester, I stress that in tribal societies the uncertainties of anxiety about crops, about the survival of children, about the growth of the young to manhood, about movements of villages, about the changes of the seasons, become intricately involved in social relations themselves; and it is this ritualization of social relations which is my problem here. The Swazi believe that their national prosperity is involved in the movement of the sun between the solstices—as indeed it is: but they believe also that the king must race the new moon to his ceremonies, as he races his subjects to 'bite' the new crops.

I think it is true to say that most roles and relationships in tribal life have considerable ceremonial attached to them, in the form of at least a highly marked code of special etiquette, the observance of social distance, and/or the avoiding of subjects in conversation. These special modes of behaviour attach to various relationships in different tribes, and tribes as a whole ceremonialize their relationships to different degrees. This is true also of changes in status. In some tribes this ceremonial—or ceremoniousness—passes markedly into ritual, as among the Tsonga, while in other tribes it does not. I have not worked on this problem sufficiently, but it does appear to me that there is some correlation between the amount of ritualization and the extent of secular differentiation in various tribes.[1] As my colleagues have given me the opportunity to introduce their essays, I throw out an idea which I have been milling over for years, without having the time to pursue it thoroughly, or the space here to set out its many implications. I do clearly see the tribal situation as standing in sharp contrast with most situations in modern industrialized and urban life. Rural life, and life in some closely knit communities such as mining villages, may still have the customs, and indeed taboos, which segregate roles.[2]

I am further prepared boldly to advance the following propositions, since, whether right or wrong, they may stimulate research into the variation in the ritualization of different tribal societies:

(a) the greater the secular differentiation of role, the less the ritual; and the greater the secular differentiation, the less mystical is the ceremonial of etiquette;

(b) the greater the multiplicity of undifferentiated and overlapping roles, the more the ritual to separate them.

In putting these propositions forward, I draw attention to the importance of specialized ritual relations in forming linkages across discrete groups with particularistic interests, as among the Tallensi[3] and the Plateau Tonga of Northern Rhodesia,[4] in the absence of more developed governmental systems, and perhaps even of age sets.[5] I have been recently impressed by the widespread effect in New Guinea of taboo against a person eating a pig, which he and his close

[1] See, e.g., my suggestion why Barotse as against Zulu and Swazi do not have elaborate political rituals, in Gluckman (1954), p. 30.

[2] See C. M. Arensberg and S. T. Kimball (1940); Arensberg (1938); and N. Dennis, F. Henriques and C. Slaughter (1956).

[3] Fortes (1945) and (1949a). See also Fortes (1959).

[4] E. Colson (1962).

[5] I make this point to acknowledge the stimulus I have had from S. Eisenstadt (1956), and from papers he read at Manchester before its publication.

relatives have bred, on the wider integration of social relations.

I have stated the truism that any ceremonial—indeed, any act of etiquette—marks the fact that a man is playing a particular role. As a worker he may doff his cap to his employer: he does not doff his cap to his child, for as a father he is superior and may keep his head covered. Hence a fortiori ceremonies at birth and at social puberty and at marriage state publicly the roles that an individual is about to play in a new context of social relations: beyond that, as Fortes shows, these ceremonies invest him with legitimate authority to play that role, by incorporating him in the status—'aggregating' him to it, in Van Gennep's terms. What I think has been inadequately appreciated is that in the very conditions of a large city, looked at in contrast with tribal society, the various roles of most individuals are segregated from one another since they are played on different stages. Thus as a child matures he moves out of the home to infant school, primary school, and secondary school, and within each of these phases he moves from class to class. Each year of his growth is marked by this progress; and each time he advances a step, he moves, within a distinctive educational building, from one room to another. Then in one stream he progresses through higher educational institutions, housed in their own buildings, to work as a salary-earner; or, in another stream, he goes through apprenticeship, or as a juvenile employee, into his role as wage-earner. Work goes on in offices and factories, in quite distinctive buildings from those in which most people live, worship, and seek their recreation, or participate in political life. Religious worship takes place in permanently sanctified buildings.[1] And these various activities associate

[1] Dr. M. Southwold has drawn my attention to the fact that Van Gennep emphasized a connection between movement in space and

individuals with quite different fellows: at school twins are likely to be the only members of a family in the same class; factories assemble people drawn from large areas, and so do most religious congregations. How a child behaves at school, or a man as a worker in his factory, does not immediately and directly affect familial relations, though it may well do this in the end: there is segregation of roles, and segregation of moral judgments. I believe that this is why custom and ceremonial are less well developed in modern society, save in those situations where we move to close-knit networks of relations, such as those described by Arensberg among the County Clare farmers and by Rosemary Harris in the Tyrone uplands, or by the Leeds sociologists in a Yorkshire mining village.[1] This situation may even arise in a great city like London, where persons are involved in close-knit networks, to use Bott's phrase: she shows that as the network of relations around a family is more closely knit, in the sense that its kin tend also to be its neighbours, its friends, and its members' workmates, there is a high differentiation of roles between husband and wife, which becomes standardized as 'custom'.[2]

In short, I consider that rituals of the kind investigated by

---

movements in status: 'it seems important to me that the passage from one social position to another is identified with a territorial passage . . .' (French ed., p. 275; trans., p. 192). He suggests that Van Gennep saw that these rites symbolically represented spatial separations of roles, which I state occur in fact in modern society. He adds that in taking territorial passages as his initial model Van Gennep was on to a fact of greater significance then he appreciated (see *loc. cit.*, Ch. 1).

[1] Arensberg, *op. cit.*; Harris, unpublished M.A. Thesis at London University (University College), quoted by permission; Dennis, Henriques and Slaughter, *op. cit.* Van Gennep himself stated that marriage ceremonies are least elaborated in our large cities, more so in the countryside, and most among semi-civilized peoples, who always live in small and highly cohesive groups (French ed., p. 199; trans., p. 139).

[2] E. Bott (1957). This is my own reading of her data.

Van Gennep are 'incompatible' with the structure of modern urban life. Kimball[1] says that there is no evidence that people living in a secular urbanized world have less need of ritualized expression for their transitions from one status to another, and he suggests that rites of passage draw attention to the social devices required to assist with problems of becoming male or female, of relations in the family, and of passing into old age. I believe he is here on a false trail. He is of course right when he says that individuals in these situations need help in some organized societal way: but I do not believe that it can come from the tribal type of *rites de passage*, in which social relationships are ritualized to assist persons at what are defined as crises. This kind of ceremony does not seem to evolve in the urban situation. I am well aware that there are initiations of apprentices in industry, of scholars at some schools and colleges, of graduates and Freemasons, and that confirmation and first communion mark stages by which boys and girls move into religious adulthood. But these are specialized ceremonies of initiation, which—indeed like weddings and funerals—mark changes of status, but they do not involve any ideas that the performing of prescribed actions by appropriately related persons will mystically affect the well-being of the initiands. It seems clear to me that the kind of rites of which Kimball speaks are indeed least likely to evolve for the lonely isolated people whose emotional needs may be greatest; and perhaps it is here that the support of social service workers has developed as a quite different way of handling the situation. Similarly, in his essay Fortes refers to the studies of Everett Hughes and other sociologists of how men take on the responsibilities of their professions and trades: in Hughes's book it will be seen that practices analysed there differ in kind from the ceremonial and rituals,

[1] 'Introduction' to translation of Van Gennep, at p. xvii.

37

the customs and taboos, which attach to working roles in tribal society.[1]

Ritual, and even ceremonial, tend to drop into desuetude in the modern urban situation where the material basis of life, and the fragmentation of roles and activities, of themselves segregate social roles. Etiquette and convention exist but they do not pass into that mystical association by which tribal peoples often believe that breach, default, and misdemeanour, and even vicious feeling, will bring misfortune on one's fellows, so that ritual dealing with mystical forces and beings is necessary to redress the equilibrium at any alteration of social dispositions, or to establish a new equilibrium in changed relations—in Van Gennep's terms, to achieve re-aggregation or aggregation.

This difference between the presence or absence of ritual is due to another difference between the two types of society. In modern society not only are roles segregated but also conflicts between roles are segregated. By 'conflicts' I refer here to the fact, which recent work in anthropology has emphasized, that many values, customs, loyalties, and allegiances, on which groups are based, are independent of one another and sometimes even discrepant with one another. The development of this view has a long history:[2] it is present in Radcliffe-Brown's analysis of the Andaman Islanders, though he is sometimes accused by those who do not read his full argument of working with a system of harmonious social cohesion. I consider, however, that this approach to the study of ritual and mystical values in tribal society received its major initial impetus from the 'Introduction' by Fortes and Evans-Pritchard to the collection of

---

[1] E. Hughes (1958).

[2] I think this view has developed largely independently of a similar view in sociology, save for Marxism. But Simmel and other sociologists have come to similar conclusions about society: see L. Coser (1956).

essays on *African Political Systems*.[1] In discussing why political office should have mystical attributes, they start from the fact that a fundamental conflict arises out of the common interest which society has in the fertility of fields and flocks and women, while it is precisely over fields and flocks and women that individuals come into competition and dispute. The political system represents the peace and moral order within which it is possible for individuals to strive for the good things that are also valued by society as a whole; and hence the political system is vested with a mystical value which places it beyond discussion and criticism. This summary statement is but a poor substitute for the original analysis. A radical development in the study of ritual followed, shown in Fortes's own work on the Tallensi, in Evans-Pritchard's essay on the Shilluk kingship, in Forde's 'Introduction' to *African Worlds*, in my own study of rituals of rebellion in South-east Africa.[2] Ritual was now seen as arising out of situations in which co-operating groups had to deal with radical conflicts in their very constitution. I consider that the best analysis yet written on these lines is Turner's *Schism and Continuity in an African Society*,[3] but it is well developed in Wilson's study of Nyakyusa rituals,[4] and apparent, though not clearly formulated, in Middleton's treatment of *Lugbara Religion*.[5] I now emphasize this point to advance my argument on why there is high ritualization of social relations in tribal society. I have of course over-simplified the position in these societies when I said that persons performed most activities in the same place with the

---

[1] Fortes and Evans-Pritchard (Eds.), (1940), pp. 16 f.

[2] *Op. cit.*, above, and Fortes (1945), *op. cit.* I have discussed this development more fully in the 'Introduction' to *Order and Rebellion* (1963), and put forward the theme in 'The Licence of Ritual', Chapter V of Gluckman (1955*b*).

[3] V. W. Turner (1957).   [4] Wilson (1959*a*) and (1957).

[5] Middleton (1960).

same set of fellows. In fact, it is a marked characteristic of all societies that persons belong to a series of different sub-groups and relationships which associate them with different fellows, so that their 'enemies' in one set of relations are their 'allies' in another; and a diversity of distinct ties interrelates the members of a society, each set of ties striking into the autonomy and isolated loyalty of the members of another set.[1] The members of the main sets of ties, however, are involved in the kind of multiplex relations from which I started my analysis; and it is because social rules and values, established by diverse relations, themselves move individuals and sub-groups to dispute with their fellows in their main group of allegiance, that ritual operates to cloak the fundamental conflicts set up. Turner and I think that this is the situation out of which ritual procedures develop, as against the use of empirical and rational procedures, such as judicial decision.[2] All three of the essays here have to be seen in this context: the installation of chief involves the conflict between office and incumbent, and the conflicts which inhere in his election; the Yakö associations override the cleavages within the village between patrilineal groups and between these and matrilineal affiliations; the Ndembu circumcision ceremony mobilizes both groups and categories of persons constituted on conflicting, or at least discrepant, principles. What Durkheim missed when he derived 'God' from the feeling of the pressure of society at an Australian corro-

[1] This kind of analysis is fully set out in Gluckman (1955b). See also G. Simmel (1955). For the record, I had not read Simmel when I wrote my own book. The anthropological view (I only stated it in general terms) developed in ignorance of Simmel's work, as far as I know: this gives independent confirmation of the view. I mention here also G. Bateson (1936) as a book out of the main stream of anthropology, which analyses a *rite de passage* in this kind of way, but with more complex concepts. Incidentally, he never refers to Van Gennep.

[2] See, especially, Turner, *op. cit.*, pp. 125 f.; and also M. G. Marwick (1952), p. 229 and elsewhere.

borree, was that the members of the 'congregation', assembled in unity there, were enemies of one another in many other situations.

This situation is clarified if we remember that while for analytic purposes it is essential to isolate a man's various roles, as if he plays each role separately at one time, in real life a man does not wear and act in a particular role as if it were a suit, as Dr. Emrys Peters put it to me, in asking me to amend my analysis. A man is known and acts as the occupant of several roles, and he carries all his roles even when one happens contextually to be dominant. Thus, most strongly, a man is not at one time a friend and at another an enemy, but always both a friend and an enemy. The roles are not as segregated as we have to make them appear in analysis. Similarly, a personal mother's brother is also at the same time a member of another lineage or, indeed, as Peters expounds it, a Bedouin mother's brother may also be an agnate and an affine, since they practise parallel cousin marriage. In addition, for finer analysis it is necessary to distinguish situations in which there is ambiguity about the role a person plays, and alterations in his behaviour within the confines of this ambiguity, from situations in which there is definite change of role. We have also to consider the rapidity with which the roles are changed, as well as the kinds of roles involved, in order to assess what influences the degree of ritualization. Professor Forde in a penetrating commentary on my manuscript made similar points when he asked me to distinguish between the multiplicity of one person's roles in relation to diverse others, and the multiple purposes involved in one person's relationship with a single other person. He went on to point out that there are several different kinds of questions involved in my essay: the continuous ritualized observance of status relations between particular persons and social categories, as between father and son and between men and women; ritualizations of the common interests of a social aggregate, as perhaps represented in a political office; and ritualized observances entailed in changes of activities, as between farming and hunting. These points, I believe, emphasize that there is something in my central argument, that ritualization in tribes, like social anthropological analysis, isolates roles largely by exaggerating the prescribed behaviour appropriate to each role involved. My friends' comments raise clearly problems for further analysis, which lie beyond the scope of a single essay.

Since these ritualized ceremonies, whatever their 'ostensible purpose' (Radcliffe-Brown), deal with conflicts between groups and relationships, conflicts which are established and validated by social rules themselves, we find that the actors in the ceremonies appear symbolically in those of their roles which are involved in the situation. They may directly 'act'[1] their roles, or reverse their roles as in transvestite behaviour, or represent them in some other symbolical form. Rituals in tribal societies are not thus mere congregations at which people pray: they are built out of the very texture of social relations,[2] each person having to perform symbolical actions, or undergo symbolical operations, which emphasize his role in relation to the other participants in the ceremony. Hence to understand the ritual, the anthropologist has to trace its symbolic actions and apparatus through a major range of social activities and other customs and complexes of symbols. Durkheim perceived this when in *De la division du travail social* he saw the movement of society from, inter alia, specific and traditional

[1] Note 'act' and not 'act out': the insertion of the preposition 'out' converts a sociological statement into a psychological statement. Some comments on my interpretation of ritual have made this slip (see 'Introduction' to Gluckman (1963)).

[2] This is brought out clearly in Bateson's description of *Naven, op. cit.*

ritual, to generalized, universalistic belief. For this form of organization of ritual, and of religious ceremonies like sacrifice,[1] through symbolic representation of role, is reduced to a minimum in modern society. There is worship, but not acting of roles; there may be ritualism, but there is not ritualization. Modern society has conflicts similar in kind to those of tribal society, but they are dispersed through different ranges of social relationships: disputes over political and economic issues, as over the distribution of wages and profits, do not normally enter family relations. Fragmentation of social relations isolates ranges of social conflicts from one another, as well as segregating roles. In a small-scale society, every issue may be at once a domestic, an economic, and a political crisis.

I have overstated the contrast between tribal and modern society to bring out what is a real difference, and I had to follow this procedure to make my analysis. The analysis is indeed supported by those many situations in modern life where we find 'pockets' of social relations which resemble those of tribal society in that there are 'groups' whose members live together in such a way that their relations in one set of roles directly influence their performance of other roles. We must not overlook their existence and possible significance. One type of such a society is a monastery, or convent, another an Oxford or Cambridge college. I cannot here try to re-analyse the descriptions we have of these situations: most of those I have consulted provide only incidental and inadequate data to provide material for an analysis in terms of our present problems. But something can be made of novels, and I begin by summarizing one fictional account of the sort of situations which arise in this

[1] See Hubert and Mauss, *op. cit.* The situation at sacrifices is clearly described in Evans-Pritchard (1956). See also Srinivas on the Coorgs, *op. cit.*

43

kind of group—C. P. Snow's *The Masters*. It depicts the struggle for power, and the shifting of social relationships, involved in the election of a new Master of a Cambridge college. One candidate's chances of election as Master are markedly affected by his role as husband, since his wife's character and actions are taken into account. This adds to the bitterness of the election, and of the defeat. But it is fascinating to follow how Snow, in aligning his two factions, does not divide them into two camps clearly separated on the basis of other common interests. They do not divide by stature in scholarship, or by whether they are scientists or in the humanities. Nor, at the critical time of the Spanish Civil War and the rise of Fascism, do all on the left support the radical candidate, while all on the right support the conservative. Some do follow these divisions implicit in the University and national political systems; but enough are swayed by personal liking and appreciation of character to prevent the two factions being absolutely divided. In the end they come to agreement because they do not trust the choice by the outsider, the Bishop who is College Visitor, to solve the internal crisis in the group by selecting an appropriate 'stranger' as Master. The final manœuvrings divide two pairs of close friends: the one pair, joined by their common interest in administrative problems, can clearly resume their friendship; the other pair, united by long friendship and common political views, remain alienated, for, as Simmel pointed out, the more intimate the relationship the severer the effects of a breach. Overall the Fellows can resume relations on the basis of common interests, since they have not been committed to support a candidate in divided total allegiances.[1] One wonders, if they had split along a dominant cleavage of political opinion or subject of

[1] See Coser, *op. cit.*, pp. 60–72, clarifying Simmel, *op. cit.*, pp. 22, and 44 f.

scholarship, whether they could have ever reunited again. A ceremonial—but not a ritualized—installation of the new Master allows an affirmation of acceptance and allegiance by the defeated faction, as well as his own followers; the defeated candidate shocks his colleagues by failing to appear at this first formal dinner of his rival, but makes the ceremonial gesture of inviting the rival to a first outside dinner with his wife. One is left feeling that bitterness provoked in choosing the Master will continue to rankle, for some time at least. Clearly—the point which as I have stated Kimball missed—if this kind of emotional difficulty could be helped by ritual, social institutions do not always develop where they are needed. The 'solution' is made possible because Fellows support the candidates in terms of a variety of preferences, arising from different positions in, and views on, the society as a whole, since these wider relations are not inevitably involved in the internal structure of the College.

I am pointing out that even in a group of this kind, in modern society, 'ritualization', in the sense which I have defined it, does not develop. Close living together is not enough: I have stressed the kinship linkages of tribal groups. But it may be that where the wider society attempts to take over control of all groups, as in authoritarian states, all groups are split by the same dominant cleavages; and this may explain why in these states there develop elaborate national ceremonies, which demand the attendance of all persons.

The best anthropological account I know on these problems in modern society is R. J. Frankenberg's study of a Welsh *Village on the Border*[1] of England. Frankenberg shows there how in a relatively isolated village with a tradition of community life, and whose members are interlinked by kinship, feuds between villagers involve conflicts

[1] R. J. Frankenberg (1957).

between social principles of organization. The unity of the village, to itself and against the outside world, is symbolized in certain recreational activities. As these have to be abandoned by the villagers because they become beset by feuds, the villagers feel that their difficulties, which they see partly as arising from the recreational activity, will end as they abandon the activity. They then start a new activity: hence Frankenberg suggests that these activities may be seen as social mechanisms akin to tribal rituals. But he stresses that the feuds continue, perhaps exacerbated by the quarrels which arose in running the earlier activity. Clearly this procedure does not deal with the conflicts, in the sense of settling them. But here again is the sort of situation in modern life which resembles the tribal situation I have delineated: and yet clearly ritual has not developed in relation to these specific activities.

I must pause here to make clear that I do not want to be interpreted as believing that rituals in tribal society settle conflicts. The whole point of the analysis is that they cannot do so: the conflicts are built into social life by the nature of social rules themselves. This is clearly discussed in Turner's discussion of competition for leadership in Ndembu lineages and villages: he stresses that as the rival groups continue to exist after each temporary settlement, marked though it is by ritual expressing social antagonisms, the disputes between them will continue and erupt periodically. In fact, they will do so more often than in modern society, despite ritual catharses and controls, since natural misfortunes, like illness, will be ascribed to the illdoing of witches among the villagers, or misdemeanours by villagers provoking ancestral wrath, or other mystical cause. Ritual clearly does not settle disputes or act as a long-term effective catharsis for anger or ambition. But, as Turner shows, the struggle for leadership produces a series of rituals which, in aiming at reconciling the parties, in fact may lead to temporary truces, and at times conceal the basic conflicts between competitors. Hence their 'functions' are not to be sought in their relation to emotional needs alone, but in a study of social relationships.[1]

There is one more striking example of situations in modern life which resemble those of tribal societies—the family economic enterprise, whether farm or business. Our literature is full of this theme of dispute between father and son, involved in this situation, and of the fundamental conflict involved in this confounding of familial and economic roles. I have not been able to search the accounts of family firms, and biographies, for material relevant to my theme. But from common knowledge I think I can fairly say that 'ritual' does not evolve in these situations, as it has among Irish farmers in Arensberg's descriptions, to segregate the roles of the members of the family engaged in the same economic enterprise. I suspect that in many cases highly conventional modes of behaviour, akin to ceremonial, may evolve. But I can only throw out this problem for others to study. Even here, however, we do not have the network of kinship links which are typical of tribal society; and the son in the firm is likely as he marries to live elsewhere, and to seek for his major recreations apart from his father. The emotional struggle in the firm for leadership may however be very acute. This contrasts sharply with the usual situation in modern urban life, where the son is not inevitably bound to wait to step into his father's shoes, but has many openings before him. In the family firm, as in tribal society, openings are more restricted, and most sons wait for their father's

[1] Turner's full analysis, *op. cit.* For an excellent account of how hostility is expressed at the installation of a Central African village-headman, see J. A. Barnes's section of Gluckman, Mitchell and Barnes (1949), pp. 100 f., republished in Gluckman (1963), *op. cit.*

position: Fortes in his recent Henry Myers Lecture discussed the taboos and mystical concepts connected with this situation among the Tallensi.[1] For lack of space, I mention only the reverse situation, which should also be studied from this point of view: the situation described by W. H. Whyte of American firms which try to take control of much of their executives' lives—and even wives.[2]

Nevertheless, clearly there may be other elements which account for the absence of ritual in this sort of situation. Here we must take into account the general bias of development, discussed by Durkheim in his analysis of the division of labour: if the whole social bias is against these rituals, they may be inhibited from appearing in this sort of situation. I draw attention particularly to Dr. Yonina Talmon's reports on developments in *kibbutzim* in Israel, where particularly closely related kin of different generations live and work together under an egalitarian ethos.[3] I cite this example specifically because it brings out an important point which we must bear in mind: the members of *kibbutzim* are part of a stream of 'anti-clerical' thought, and are self-conscious about their actions. Self-consciousness about the development of tribal-type rituals may inhibit them from appearing. In some ways this is arguing from the negative as well as the positive case: but I am here trying to set out problems on which not much detailed work has been done.

The difficulty about this comparison is that questions of conventional and ceremonial behaviour in Britain, at least, have not attracted the attention of sociologists. We may well ask why the Vice-Chancellors of some universities are ceremonially installed, and not others, while other important people like Ministers of the Crown or Permanent Secretaries of Governments are not? Are the reasons historical?

[1] Fortes (1961), pp. 166–89.   [2] W. H. Whyte (1956).
[3] Talmon (1959*a*), pp. 2 f.; and (1959*b*).

Why do universities vary from the elaborateness of an Oxford degree ceremony to the virtual absence of such a ceremony in London? Is this why the Lord Mayor of the City of London is installed with great ceremony, but not the Chairman of the London County Council? Why is the work of the courts of law and of judges surrounded with so much ceremony? Some answers to these problems might help our interpretation of the rituals of tribal society, whether my own hypothesis be right or wrong.

I argue[1] that it is a fact that tribal societies have a greater elaboration of ceremoniousness in all their relationships than modern society has, in the form of stylized etiquette appropriate to specific roles and relationships. This is not to deny that etiquette is found in all situations: general patterns marking superiority and subordination, or equality of status, are found everywhere. Yet there is a difference in degree which passes into a difference of kind. Durkheim touched on this problem in defining some of the attributes of those societies which are mechanically solid, as against those which are organically solid. Van Gennep dismissed the problem by relating the elaboration of tribal ceremonial to the semi-civilized mind. I spell out Durkheim's thesis by stating that in tribal societies persons play several roles in relation to others in the same environs, so that roles are not differentiated by material conditions and fragmented associations: hence we find here more specific customs of stylized etiquette, more conventions and taboos, and more custom in general, to differentiate and segregate these roles in their various sets of purposive activities. Beyond this, individuals are also required in terms of their membership of groups and relationships to act in multiplex relationships, and though they co-operate in these in several sets of purposive activity, they also are brought into competition and struggle through

[1] M. Southwold has helped me clarify my summary.

other allegiances. This total situation leads to a compound of moral evaluations on all actions, and the conflict between interwoven allegiances disturbs these evaluations. Breach of relations sets up widespread disturbance. Breach of social relations is associated with what we call natural misfortunes, and natural misfortunes are explained by derelictions from duty. Each alteration in social status or social arrangements in general is regarded as liable to disturb the natural order (even if this is not formulated by the people concerned explicitly). Hence ceremoniousness in social relations becomes involved with mystical beliefs which state that this ceremoniousness can affect the groups or persons concerned in ways that are not open to observation, by influencing their prosperity. I then speak of social relations as 'ritualized'. As Fortes shows in his essay, among the roles that receive special ritualization are roles of authority; and in tribal societies I suggest the legitimation of authority takes on a mystical character because those in authority are involved in many other relationships with their followers. This ritualization consists often in the special enactment of social duties by appropriate persons of their everyday actions, or reversal of these actions, as well as in performing special rites. In short, the ritual which deals with social status as well as with environmental events is built out of the symbolical enactment of social relations themselves.

In conclusion, I pay tribute to Radcliffe-Brown, as well as Van Gennep, a tribute with which my colleagues will gladly associate themselves, since, like me, they have learnt much from him. In his study of *The Andaman Islanders* he posed most of these problems. He saw that the ceremonial of the 'life-crises' dealt with the 'social personality' of the individual, defined as '. . . the sum of characteristics by which he has an effect upon the social life and therefore on the social sentiments of others . . .' (at p. 285). Under the influence of Durkheim and Shand he thereupon concentrated his analysis on the moral and social sentiments, rather than on social relations. He writes that 'by death the "social personality" . . . from being an object of pleasurable states of the social sentiments . . . becomes an object of painful states'. A death '. . . is a direct attack against these [social] sentiments'. Radcliffe-Brown wrote that he believed that burial customs were to be explained '. . . as a collective reaction against the attack on the collective feeling of solidarity constituted by the death of a member of the social group' (pp. 285-6). This analysis in terms of sentiments may of course be sound: but in addition, while making it, Radcliffe-Brown examined the symbolic means by which the roles of survivors are readjusted ritually to the death. Lacking the concept of roles, which has proved so important in anthropology and sociology, he did not adequately break up the social personality, which is a cluster of roles, into its component parts, and trace thoroughly how each was readjusted. But he stated the problem as clearly as might be at the time. I myself applied his concept to Junod's material on the Tsonga, and suggested that a fieldworker might find it profitable to examine a funeral, not only in terms of the status of the deceased, but also as a situation which varied for all the different persons involved, whether widow, son, brother, chief, dependant, or other person; and thus (though I did not put it in these terms) one could elaborate on the readjustment and alteration of roles involved.[1] Unfortunately, when I myself became a fieldworker, my own interests lay in different directions, and I happened to study peoples who had little ritualization: the Zulu had lost theirs,[2] the

[1] Gluckman (1937), pp. 117 f.
[2] The Zulu have very many rituals, with a few elements of what I have called 'ritualization', in their separatist sects: see B. Sundkler (1948 and 1961).

Barotse never had much ritual. I believe too that I have a temperamental incapacity for the detailed 'social histology' (as Fortes has named it for me) required for this kind of work. I mention my early article here, for I consider that by studying ceremonies in this way we would learn much: some of the answers are set out in the essays which follow.

Secondly, Radcliffe-Brown wrote of the Andaman Islanders: 'The social life is a process of complex interaction of powers or forces present in the society itself, in each individual, in animals and plants and the phenomena of nature, and on these powers the well-being of the society and its members depends . . . The ceremonial of the Andaman Islanders may be said to involve the assumption of a power of a peculiar kind. . . . This power, though in itself neither good nor evil, is the source of all good and evil in social life. It is present in the society and in everything that can affect in important ways the social life' (p. 307 f.). He considered the feeling of this power to be a real experience (p. 325), and spoke of the hostility or opposition or antagonism between society and nature, between customary duty and selfish inclination, between individual and society, between group and group. The step he did not take definitely enough was to see that society is compounded of multiple groups and relationships, whose allegiances strike into one another, and that men make their living in links of co-operation and conflict enjoined by social rules themselves. But he made that step possible.

If our essays advance our knowledge, it is because we start from the points which men like Van Gennep and Radcliffe-Brown reached after hard marching.

RITUAL AND OFFICE
IN TRIBAL SOCIETY

by MEYER FORTES

Theoretical Preliminaries

FEW concepts in the vocabulary of sociology and social anthropology are so lavishly used as are 'role' and 'status'. Since they were first put into regular circulation by Linton[1] they have been the subject of discussion from many angles of theory,[2] some within but most, perhaps, beyond the customary range of social anthropology. It is as well, therefore, that I need say little about this literature. For I am not concerned with elucidating definitions. What I want to consider is how the kinds of attributes, capacities and relationships which we identify by means of such terms are generated, more particularly in a tribal society. I do not have to emphasize that this is a well-worn theme in anthropology. Some of our most illustrious forbears, presently to be mentioned, have explored it. And what I have to say is of value mainly as a reminder of how much still remains to be followed up in their theories and discoveries. I was tempted to take it up again in this lecture because it has been on my mind for some time[3] and it seemed to fit in well with the aim of this series.

[1] Ralph Linton (1936).
[2] Parsons and Nadel, cited later, review some of this literature. See also the thought-provoking paper by A. Southall (1959), pp. 17 ff. An unusual point of view is expounded with subtlety and wit in Erving Goffman (1959).
[3] A preliminary draft of this paper was written during my tenure of a Fellowship at the Center for Advanced Study in the Behavioral Sciences, Stanford, California, and benefited greatly from the comments of several colleagues at the Center.

Colloquially speaking, terms like role and status help us to isolate and analyse the parts played by people in social life. They have status in domestic, local, political, religious, etc. groups, associations, classes; they exercise roles in economic, legal, ritual, military, conjugal, etc. relationships. And we use this terminology to show that what we are talking about is customary, or standard, or normal—institutionalized, if you will.

This is elementary. What is fundamental, however, is that roles and statuses must be legitimate in the society in which they occur; that is to say, they must have moral and jural sanction. Parsons[1] showed this neatly by reference to the 'legitimacy' of sickness as against criminality in our own society. A person does not just step into a role or acquire a status as he might a garment. They are, as Nadel remarks,[2] allotted to, or rather conferred upon him by society.

But how, when, in what circumstances? Confronted with this question, an anthropologist immediately thinks of the roles and statuses which, in Linton's terminology, are achieved and which stand out as palpably conferred. Some appear to accrue to a person at successive stages of the normal life cycle and the basic achievement might well be considered to be staying the course from birth through childhood, adolescence, adulthood and so on.

This, essentially, is the theme of Van Gennep's famous study of *rites de passage*.[3] In setting up what we should now call his model of the standard and, to all intents, universal life cycle, Van Gennep demonstrated three significant theorems: first, that the critical stages, as he called them, of the life cycle, beginning with birth and going on to puberty, marriage, parenthood, and finally death, though tied to physio-

[1] Talcott Parsons (1951), especially Chs. VII and X.
[2] S. F. Nadel (1957), p. 35.
[3] Van Gennep, *op. cit.*

logical events, are in fact socially defined;[1] secondly, that entry into and exit from these critical stages—or statuses— are always marked by ritual and ceremony, not only in primitive societies but equally in Christian civilization and in the civilizations of antiquity; thirdly, that these passage rites follow a more or less standard pattern. They begin with rites of separation, which remove the subject from the 'environment' or as we might say social field he is in, then come transition rites, while the subject is, so to speak, waiting on the threshold of the status or social field he is about to enter, and finally come rites of incorporation into the new status.

Van Gennep's model has become so entrenched in our thinking that it is seldom explicitly questioned; and rightly so, for it represents one of the major theoretical achievements of our science. Yet the most important questions are left in the air by him, though pregnant suggestions for dealing with them are thrown out in the course of his analysis. Thus the crucial question, why is ritual apparently indispensable in marking status change, is not pursued in detail. It is deemed to be accounted for, partly, by the hypothesis that progression from one stage to the next is commonly a change from a profane to a sacred environment or situation. But this proves to be a Procrustean formula when, for example, initiation rites are in one place summed up as 'rites of separation from the usual environment, rites of incorporation into the sacred environment; a transitional period; rites of separation from the local sacred environment; rites of incorporation into the usual environment'.[2] In addition, there

---

[1] E.g. 'It is apparent that the physiological return from childbirth is not the primary consideration, but that instead there is a *social return from childbirth*, just as there is a social parenthood which is distinct from physical parenthood, and a social marriage which is distinct from sexual union. We will see that there is also a social puberty which does not coincide with physical puberty' (*op. cit.*, trans., p. 46).

[2] Van Gennep, *op. cit.*, p. 82.

is the implication that ritual is appropriate because it mimes or symbolizes the nature of the passage in each particular case. A simple instance is the interpretation of 'rites which involve cutting something' . . . the first haircut, the shaving of the head . . . '—as rites of separation, whereas naming and baptism are obvious rites of incorporation'. Other interpretations offered are more subtle; but inspired as some of them are, they mostly remain at the level of manifest meaning I have exemplified.[1] Again, Van Gennep makes acute comparisons between passage rites marking status stages in the life cycle and passage rites by which people are initiated and incorporated into secret societies, cult groups, age-groups, offices, ranks and even the world of the dead. There is the brilliant observation that even where membership in a caste, class or cult group is hereditary, 'the child is rarely considered a fully "complete" member from birth . . . he must be incorporated'; and he adds, casually, that in these ceremonies the 'politico-legal' and 'social' elements are more important than the magico-religious. All the same, the point we would follow up is not considered. If we generalize the model, attaining a status that is normal to the life cycle is equivalent to admission to membership in a closed association and these are equivalent to entering upon an office or rank, and to passing into the society of the dead; and the critical step is the rite of incorporation. If we ask, incorporation into what, the answer is clear: into a new field of social structure, or conjuncture of social relations.

But why ritual? A clue lies in turning from the procedures of conferring it, to the recipient of status, role or office. The actor, docile though he may be while undergoing the

[1] *Op. cit.*, p. 53. But I do not want to minimize the extraordinary insight displayed in Van Gennep's interpretations. An example is his description of initiation rites at adolescence as rites of separation from the asexual world followed by rites of incorporation into the world of sexuality (p. 67).

process of being incorporated, lives and acts the part once he possesses it. He appropriates his part to himself, he knows it, he has a commitment to it. It is through the acting of his part in accordance with the norms and sanctions that legitimize it that he is incorporated in the social structure. This has been recognized by theoretical writers like Parsons, Nadel and others. What needs to be particularly pointed out is that there is a dialectical connection between the actor and his part, the person and his roles or status or office. He is made to appropriate his part to himself because it is in a sense outside himself. This emerges, I think, from the ethnographic evidence presently to be adduced. I believe that this is where the clue to the need for ritual and ceremony in status-giving lies.

It is, of course, not a novel hypothesis. It follows from the analysis of what is meant by the concept of 'office' which I regard as the generic term embracing role and status as special cases. Its significance was first brought home to me, as, no doubt, to most of us, by Max Weber's classical exposition of the notion of 'calling' (or its equivalent in German, *Beruf*) in Protestant ethical and theological teaching.[1] As Parsons sums it up elsewhere,[2] it is 'the conception of an individual's "business in life" . . . as a matter of moral obligation' which, as Weber emphasizes, derives its sanctions from the will of God. Weber's *Beruf* is equated with and translated appropriately by 'calling', 'occupation', 'profession', 'life-task' and 'office' in different parts of his work; but 'office' is, I consider, by its etymology, history and connotation the correct general term.

It is not within my competence, nor indeed is this the place, to go into the history of the notion of 'office' from its

[1] Max Weber (1930), Ch. III, and (1947), Ch. II, sec. 14, 24, *et passim*.
[2] Parsons, 'Introduction' to M. Weber (1947), p. 72, and (1937), Chs. 14–15.

Roman origins until today.¹ Weber attributes its development, in the sense he gives to it, primarily to Martin Luther. It arose, as Dr. Cargill Thompson shows in a forthcoming book,² from Luther's rigorous distinction between 'the spiritual, inner new man' and the 'carnal, external, old man'.

Thus the concept of office is not an artifice of modern sociological theory. In my view it is so essential to the management and comprehension of the social relations of persons and groups that it is present in all social systems, if only in an embryonic form. In Africa, for example, the distinction between the man himself and the office he occupies is as well understood as it is amongst us today and in earlier periods of European history. It is a common concept in African political constitutions, and is deeply ingrained in

¹ It is however worth noting that *officium*, the ancestral form of our word, was used by the Romans, e.g. Cicero and Seneca, in much the same sense as Weber's *Beruf*. It is commonly translated as 'moral duty', and 'occupation'. But it was used also to denote ritual and ceremony associated with induction into status, rank and office, e.g. marriage, the assumption of the *toga virilis*, entry upon magisterial office. Cf. Georges (1959), *s.v. cit.*

² I am indebted to Dr. W. D. J. Cargill Thompson, King's College, Cambridge, for permission to quote him on this subject. 'Luther contrasted the "spiritual, inner, new man" with the "carnal, external, old man" (Luther, *De Libertate Christiana*). Good works could not win salvation because they are performed by the outward natural man, not by spiritual man. Man's two natures involve him in one set of relationships with God and in another with his fellow-men. These Luther called two "callings" (*vocatio, Beruf*), or "persons" (Christ-person and *Welt-person*) or offices (*Ampt*). In his spiritual calling a man is incorporated in Christ through the Word and baptism; in his temporal calling he has offices to serve the needs of mankind, and this may require him to do things that are expressly forbidden to him as a private Christian. Thus as a magistrate, a preacher, a slave or especially as a soldier who is bound to fight or as a parent bound to exercise authority over his children, he is under obligations to his temporal office. As the temporal order is also instituted by God, it is incumbent on a man not to disrupt it by refusing to serve in the office to which he has been called' (Cargill Thompson, 'The Two Regiments').

African legal institutions, moral values, and jural norms. I do not have to labour this point in Manchester, since no one here can be unfamiliar with its exposition and elucidation in Professor Gluckman's analysis of the judical process among the Barotse. At the outset of his book[1] he establishes the importance of separating the offices of the court-councillors from their holders, and as the argument proceeds we see how this fits in with the cardinal principle of Lozi jurisprudence, that courts 'deal with an individual person occupying specific positions in society' (p. 198); they are 'chiefly concerned with relationships of status' (p. 126).

Office, *par excellence*, is seen in chiefship and other forms of constituted political leadership, as well as in similarly established positions of authority in economic or religious or otherwise institutionalized activities. Ashanti chiefship exemplifies a way of recognizing the distinction I am discussing that is particularly apt for my purpose. The office is referred to by the term *akonnua*, commonly translated 'stool' in the same way as we use 'crown' and 'throne' to stand for Kingship. The culminating rite of the installation ceremony is the solemn seating of the chief-elect on the supreme ancestral stool of his chiefdom. From this moment he is obliged to observe a number of rigorous taboos and is regarded as 'invested with sanctity', as Rattray puts it.[2] Appearing then, before his people, he swears fidelity to them and is admonished by his senior councillors to remember, among other things, that he may never act without their advice, and must rule with justice and impartiality. It is impressed on him that he belongs to the whole chiefdom in his capacity as chief, and not to his lineage. The office is deemed to absorb the whole person during his tenure of it. Thus any treasure a chief takes with him when he is installed becomes part of the stool property, and any territory, persons or valuables he is

[1] Gluckman (1955a).   [2] See R. S. Rattray (1929), Ch. XI.

instrumental in winning during his tenure of the stool accrue to the office.

As is well known, Ashanti constitutional law permits the councillors of a chiefdom who elect and install a chief to demand his abdication or to depose him if he offends against the laws and customs, fails in his duties, or commits sacrilege.[1] When this happens the chief is destooled by a ceremony that reverses the enstoolment rites. His sandals are removed so that he steps barefoot on the earth and his buttocks are bumped on the ground by the withdrawal of his stool from under him. Thus he transgresses two of the symbolic taboos of chiefship and is deemed to have degraded his sacred office. He is then banished, accompanied by only one wife and a servant. He is now a commoner member of his lineage again and is no longer treated with the reverential deference accorded to a chief. He can keep none of the properties or treasure or, nowadays, the money and clothes, which accrued to his office during his chiefship. In recent times this has been a source of grievance and litigation, for chiefs have been able to exploit their official authority and prestige to enrich themselves on the side, in the cocoa trade, by traffic in concessions and land rentals, by money-lending and so forth. Litigation has not infrequently taken place between a destooled chief and his former councillors and subjects over the disposal of such gains. Traditional constitutional law regards them as belonging to the Stool. But suits are brought on the basis of British laws of property and persons, and courts have sometimes ruled that a chief's capacity as a private citizen is not extinguished by his assumption of office. This entitles him to claim his private property and possessions irrespective of when they were gained.[2]

[1] K. A. Busia (1951), Ch. II; Rattray (1929), *op. cit.*, pp. 116–17.
[2] It would be interesting to pursue this topic further, especially in relation to Gluckman's previously cited study. But it impinges on an

I have dwelt on this instance because it brings me back to a feature of office which Weber hardly considered and Van Gennep only partly investigated. I mean the part played by ceremony and ritual, not only in the conferment of office but also in its maintenance and exercise. And lest we should be inclined to think that this holds only for primitive society, I would draw attention to the perceptive and ingenious studies of various professions and occupations carried out over a period of years by Professor Everett Hughes and his collaborators.[1] 'Status', says Hughes (and I concur), 'is an elementary form of office', which he defines as a 'standardized group of duties and privileges devolving upon a person in certain well defined situations'—I would rather say, in customarily defined and sanctioned contexts of social relations. But what is most to the point in these studies is the observation that for the office represented in a profession like medicine or the law—and even in an occupation as low in our scale of class esteem as that of a janitor or dustman— to be fittingly exercised needs a 'mandate from society' given through its responsible organs and institutions. Thus it

---

aspect of office which can only be alluded to here. I mean the connection between the concept of office and the juridical concept of the 'corporation sole'. A jurist, I take it, would say that office is none other than the corporation sole in another guise. There is authority for this in English constitutional history. If we turn to the fountain-head, we find that the question comes up in Pollock and Maitland (1898) in connection with issues that are closely parallel to the conflicts of status illustrated by Ashanti chiefship. Thus (Vol. I, p. 495) they discuss the difficulties of sixteenth-century lawyers over the king's status. Was he to be regarded as 'merely a natural person' or also as an 'ideal person', a 'corporation sole'? They conclude that the 'personification of the kingly office in the guise of a corporation sole was, in the then state of the law, an almost necessary expedient'. And they refer back to a much earlier state of affairs when there was no clear-cut distinction between the king's proprietary rights as king and those he had in his private capacity (*ibid.*, pp. 502–3).

[1] Everett C. Hughes (1958), especially pp. 56 ff.

becomes 'licensed', or legitimate. It is this fact which determines how an office appears to its holder, how he apprehends the duties and privileges it entails, and how he fulfils them.

Here the ceremonial and ritual elements become specially relevant. Should we follow Van Gennep and say that the key lies in the phenomenon that office, status and roles are always conferred by *rites de passage* which move a person from a profane to a sacred setting and state? This, as I have already implied, is much too facile. We see this if we state the thesis in the more enlightening concepts developed by Robert Redfield in his notable analysis of the relationships between the 'technical order' and the 'moral order' in civilization.[1] What office, status or role is there which does not serve some instrumental or utilitarian—that is technical, end? And yet there is always also this other dimension of duty and responsibility, enjoined, sanctioned, and above all symbolized in ceremonial or ritual forms (be it no more than costume and etiquette) placing it in the moral order. This is as obvious in the western professions described by Hughes as in African tribal life. But being primarily concerned with and interested in the latter, I will now turn to some of the evidence from ethnography.

Ethnographical Observations

I remember the first time I saw a procession of mourners on their way to a funeral among the Tallensi. They included both men and women, dressed in gala clothes and carrying condolence gifts of guinea corn and chickens. A drummer and a fiddler escorted them. As they hove in sight, they were carrying on an animated conversation, laughing and joking. A bystander praised their admirable turnout. This, he said, was the proper way to attend the funeral of your father-in-law. All of a sudden the procession halted. Then, as

[1] Robert Redfield (1953).

it began to move forward again, a heart-rending wail broke forth. It came from the women. Tears were now streaming down their cheeks; and, as their wailing swelled, the men joined in with a melancholy dirge. In this way they arrived at the house of the bereaved family. What was the meaning of this transformation of mien and mood? Was it sincere or were the players simply putting on an act for which they were cast in their capacity as the kinsfolk of a son-in-law fulfilling a kinship obligation? I often discussed this question with Tallensi. Invariably they insisted that the wailing and the dirges expressed sincere grief. This, they insisted, is the customary mode of expressing condolence by a son-in-law's kin. How else could the mourners have shown their grief? Are there not, they went on, appropriate times, places and occasions for people to act in the customary ways that show the world that one is a kinsman or an affine or just a good friend? Mourners attending an in-law's funeral do not give vent to grief in their own home settlements. The appropriate place is the bereaved clan settlement.

Here we see how occasions evoke, and thus confer roles, according to standard patterns. But this occurrence is fully intelligible only if we take into account the whole context of status relationships implicit in it. A man has unrestricted rights over his wife's reproductive capacity in virtue of the bride-price he has paid to her father. But she never wholly forfeits her status as her father's daughter. This gives her residual claims on her father's protection and him a lien on her. If her marriage is unsuccessful she can, with her father's support, escape from it. A son-in-law is therefore in the perpetual debt of his father-in-law, being dependent on his goodwill, first for the original gift of his daughter, later for backing in maintaining the marriage. To mourn for his father-in-law is one of a number of customary demonstrations of respect he is obliged to make throughout his married life. If he inexcusably neglects these duties his wife's paternal kin may assert their rights and take her away. Jural right is here backed by moral justification. For people will say: how can a man be so callous towards his wife's feelings or so deficient in a sense of duty and propriety as wilfully to fail in his affinal obligations? The status of son-in-law carries with it not only rights and duties but also attitudes and sentiments, as shown, *inter alia*, by the appropriate mourning behaviour for an affine. We should note that a respectable son-in-law takes pride in this. It reaffirms the affinal relations created by his marriage and this is tantamount to advertising the rights he holds and making acknowledgement of the obligations incurred.

Let me state the conclusion prompted by this example in what might be thought to be somewhat far-fetched terms; but I think it will help to advance the discussion. Firstly, roles, even transient ones, are only evoked in persons who may legitimately exercise them—nay must, in certain circumstances, do so; and secondly, roles are performed not automatically, but in response to social controls that emanate from the relationships in which the roles emerge.[1] For what, in fact, is the capacity to take on a role other than the manifestation of engagement in social relations? If role is status in action then status is shorthand for everything that is required of a person or permitted to him in virtue of a specified field of social relations in which he is involved. This point, sometimes overlooked in theoretical discussions, is well made in the paper by Southall previously cited. So to establish precisely what the status of son-in-law implies we must specify that it belongs to the domestic domain of social structure.[2]

But status in this domain is less instructive for my pur-

[1] As Parsons fully explains in *The Social System* (1951).
[2] See my introduction to Goody (Ed.), Ch. I (1958).

pose than its counterpart in the external domains of the political and the religious order. Let us therefore consider more fully what I have called office *par excellence*. To make my description clear I must remind you that the Tallensi have no indigenous political institutions of the type we associate with centralized government. Without courts of law, administration or over-riding authorities, the sovereignty of the exogamous, patrilineal local clan is kept in check partly by the complex web of kinship created by marriage but chiefly by an elaborate scheme of ritual interdependence. With a segmentary political system and with subsistence farming as their only source of livelihood, they have no framework of unity in the technical order of their culture. What political and moral cohesion they have arises from public ritual institutions.[1] And the pivotal institutions are focused in the two hereditary offices of the Chiefship, vested in one group of clans, and the Custodianship of the Earth, vested in another group, as I have described fully elsewhere.[2]

To summarize very briefly, the founding myth of the tribe tells how the chiefly clans entered the country as immigrants bringing the Chiefship with them, and came to live among the aboriginals who constituted the Earth-priest clans. A compact was then established which bound the two groups for ever to live in amity side by side. Neither group has any authority over the other, and indeed the Chiefs and Earth-priests have no powers comparable to what we would call political authority even in their own groups. But Chiefs and Earth-priests are bound to one another by complementary religious and mystical observances, ties and duties;

[1] These topics are dealt with at length in my article 'The Political System of the Tallensi', in Fortes and Evans-Pritchard (1940).

[2] See Fortes (1945). I use the slightly inexact term 'Earth-priest' in the present discussion to save circumlocution and confusing recourse to native words.

for the two sets of offices are primarily religious, not technical, in Redfield's sense of these terms. The Tallensi believe that the common good of the whole tribe depends on the faithful ritual collaboration of Chiefs and Earth-priests, after the fashion, as they put it, of husband and wife. If this breaks down, famine, war, disease or some other catastrophe will descend on them. And an essential rule governing this complementary politico-religious relationship is that the two sets of offices are mutually exclusive. The clans eligible for one set are barred from the other. In fact the distinctive attributes of each of the offices derives from its complementary opposition to the other in the tribal system. This is documented and demonstrated through the medium of ritual observances. A Chief, and anyone who is eligible for the office by clan descent, may wear cloth, ride a horse, and use firearms. Earth-priests and their clansmen may not do any of these things. They must wear animal skins, and may not ride a horse or use a firearm on pain of mystical punishment by the Earth. A Chief may not tread the bare earth unshod. Earth-priests may and do. A Chief may not eat certain animals permitted to ordinary people and to Earth-priests. And there are other ritual injunctions and prohibitions of these kinds binding on both. All these ritual rules are justified by appeal to the founding myth.

* * *

Let us note that it is not enough for the offices to exist and to have what in present sociological parlance is often designated by the ponderous but indispensable word 'incumbents'. The holders must be dressed for their parts, so to speak, and must show that they are living their parts by observing a number of distinctive and often onerous ritual restrictions which have no rational justification, let alone utility, but only the sanction of myth and religious belief.

This of course is not confined to the Tallensi, or to the many other African peoples who have similar institutions.[1] It is characteristic of office anywhere. Office needs must be distinguished, on the one hand by outward and visible trappings, and on the other by characteristic modes of conduct. Hughes (*op. cit.*) has pointed this out. The evidence is all around us, in our police and bus conductors, in the professions and the churches, in courts of law, universities, banks, industry, business, wherever office occurs. But what is brought home to us by a consideration of positions of rank and authority in a tribal society like that of the Tallensi is that these emblems and insignia are associated with distinctive norms of conduct and observance which symbolize jural capacities and responsibilities and bind those who hold an office to it by ritual sanctions. And what I want to fix attention on is that this is the result of a social act of investment by a deliberate and formal procedure.

I am, of course, referring to the well-known fact that a chief or similar functionary in any African society is invariably installed in office by a public ceremony. The Ashanti ceremony has already been mentioned. Among the Tallensi, it is an elaborate and solemn ceremony which includes a number of esoteric rites. For both of the politico-ritual offices it begins with rites which confer on the holder the apparel and other insignia of his office. These are followed by the more esoteric rites which can best be understood as imposing on him his taboos and other ritual observances. And their import is clear; they confer a new social identity on the holder, symbolized by his taking a new name. This

[1] I have already noted some of the taboos of office that fall upon an Ashanti chief. He is subject to many other constraints of conduct and observance which I have not the space to discuss but which are described in the literature cited. Anthropologists hardly need to be reminded that this is characteristic of chiefship all over Africa and in other parts of the world. To list relevant references would be out of place here.

was vividly impressed on me when I attended the installation of a senior Earth-priest. Almost overnight, an ineffectual old man was turned into a dignified, self-confident, and authoritative, if somewhat garrulous, leader.

Tallensi assert that if Chiefs and Earth-priests fail in their duties, whether these appear to be secular or are clearly religious, they are transgressing their taboos; and disasters will surely come upon the whole country. Is it then simply superstitious fears that constrain them to fulfil their tasks and obligations, as a superficial judgment might suggest? To answer this question we must look more closely at the relationship between an office-holder and his office. In the first place, the office must be occupied. Tallensi give many instances of how crops withered unaccountably and disease spread through the country during the interregnum between the death of one Chief or priest and the installation of his successor. I more than once heard a Chief upbraid a group of difficult litigants by reminding them that if he were to lay down his office in anger over their recalcitrance, the rains would fail or other disasters immediately fall on the whole country.[1] The office, as such, is otiose, or rather anomalous and therefore dangerous to society, unless it is occupied.

Here we touch again on a point of principle mentioned briefly before. An unoccupied politico-ritual office endangers the stability of social life because law and order, personal security, and ultimately man's relations with nature, are jeopardized by the absence of the king-pin of the social structure. Blackstone's maxim that 'the King

[1] This, again, is a familiar religious (more correctly, cosmological) concomitant of eminent politico-ritual office in Africa. It is most dramatically represented in the well-known institution of Divine Kingship. (Cf. the excellent synopsis in Evans-Pritchard (1948).) The elaborate development of this conception in ancient Egypt is brilliantly expounded by Henri Frankfort (1948).

never dies' sums up the central issue. Offices of the type represented by chiefship and kingship may not lapse or be dissolved if the society is to be maintained as it is: and it is they that constitute corporations sole in their juridical aspect. The significant structural index of this is the fact that they entail succession. To be sure the duties and privileges of the office may be temporarily fulfilled during its vacancy by some kinsman or representative of the successor-apparent, or of the group that possesses it. But succession by due process, to borrow a phrase normally used with a rather different implication, must ensue, else there is discord, perhaps revolution. In fact the chaos of the interregnum, often accompanied by wars of succession, is, paradoxically, accepted as inevitable in some societies.

This used to happen among the Tallensi and peoples related to them (e.g. the Mamprussi). Tallensi say that in the old days, when a major chief died the 'land fell to pieces' with famine and rapine and did not recover until a successor had been installed. Ashanti say that a vacant stool is repugnant to custom because there is nobody to take care of the ancestral stools and to offer libations and sacrifices to them. This is ominous for peace and social well-being. Indeed in some chiefdoms the danger of chaos during the interregnum after the death of a chief is magically averted by the seizure of the chiefly sacra by the hereditary controllers of the obsequies.[1] There is a curious parallelism between this practice and the rituals of rebellion described by Gluckman.[2] Among the Mossi the interregnum between the demise of a King and the selection and installation of his successor is stabilized by one of those neat devices that delight anthropologists. Immediately upon the death of a King his eldest daughter is dressed in his robe of office and, holding

[1] These are the *wirempefo* referred to by Rattray (1927), Ch. XVIII.
[2] Gluckman (1954).

his staff, is seated on the royal skin to hold court daily until the funeral is over and one of her brothers is installed as the new ruler. Thus the office is kept warm, as it were, by a member of the royal lineage who is barred by her sex from the succession and from transmitting it to her sons but is qualified by descent to represent the lineage in safeguarding its title and the stability of the social order against the possibility of civil war over the succession.[1] The problem was dealt with as ingeniously in ancient Egypt. As Frankfort explains (*op. cit.*, Ch. VIII), the Egyptian solution was to appoint the heir-apparent co-regent with his father, the reigning king. He acceded to power immediately on his father's death but it was not until the conclusion of the coronation ritual that the danger of rebellion by pretenders was over.

It boots not to multiply the examples which abound in Africa. Wherever this type of office is found the death of a ruler is a major crisis. As J. D. and E. J. Krige put it, in writing of the Lovedu,[2] it 'dislocates the rhythm of nature, bringing drought and famine, the abrogation of law and order'. At best there is a state of public suspense and minor lawlessness, at worst the anarchy of a struggle for the succession by rival claimants. And order does not return until the office is revivified by legitimate reoccupation.

* * *

It is hardly to be wondered at that the installation of the successor so commonly includes elaborate ritual and ceremony, not only in order that he might be incontestably proclaimed but also in order that the bonds of office that bind

[1] I infer this from the remarkable ethnographic film of 'The Installation of the Mogho Na'aba' shown by Dr. Jean Rouch at the Sixth International Congress of Anthropological Sciences, Paris, 1960.

[2] J. D. and E. J. Krige, 'The Lovedu of the Transvaal' in Forde (Ed.), (1954).

the holder to those for whom he holds it may be irre-
fragably forged. Furthermore, the installation rites commonly devolve, as right and duty, on a special group of
'king-makers'. These are often, if not usually, hereditary
councillors of the ruler, some at least being holders of
priestly or religious office connected with sacred places or
relics or shrines of the ruler's office, or else with his ritual
obligations. And it is a cardinal rule that these electors must
not themselves be eligible for the succession, nor may those
who can succeed to the ruler's office hold an elector's office.[1]
The Tallensi maxim 'Nobody installs himself' puts it
succinctly. Lineage heads, whether Chiefs or Earth-priests,
are installed by neighbouring lineage heads whose clans have
the hereditary privilege of performing this task.[2] The
electors are, in effect, the agents of the tribe and the custodians of the body of law and custom. It is in the name of the
people, and of the sancity of this body of law and custom,
that they confer office on a ruler. This is dramatized in
installation ceremonies.

But before I say more about these, I would like to draw
attention to a corollary of the foregoing argument. I have
used chiefship as the model of office *par excellence*. But it is,
of course, only a pre-eminent instance of a type of office or
status found also in other domains of social life. The defining structural criteria—that the office may not be left unoccupied, that it is, in consequence, perpetuated by succession, and that the holder, though chosen by virtue of prior
title, must nevertheless be ritually invested with it by the
agents of society—are also met by other institutions. The
instances that come to mind are the 'positional succession'

[1] An idea of course familiar to us from English and European history.
[2] In Ashanti the selection and installation of a chief are the jealously
guarded prerogatives of the Queen Mother and the councillors. See
Rattray (1929), *passim*, and Busia, *op. cit.*

and 'perpetual kinship' practised by some Central African peoples.[1] But as a matter of fact, it is evident, in however rudimentary a form, wherever succession, as opposed to inheritance, is mandatory. Among the Tallensi a man's property passes by inheritance partly to his lineage brothers and partly to his sons. But his jural status as head of his family, wielding paternal authority, passes by succession to his oldest son, who is ritually invested with it in the concluding rites of his funeral.[2] It might be thought that there is an element of this in all status in a homogeneous and relatively stable society. But we can see that this is not so if we contrast the status of a son-in-law with which we began. This cannot be attained by succession, but only by marriage. Again, the status of initiated man or marriageable woman, which figures so prominently in the normal model of *rites de passage*, is not attainable by succession.

I must refrain from following this point further and return to installation ceremonies. Their resemblance to initiation rites was stressed by Van Gennep and their general pattern is known to all. One way of putting it would be to say that these rites extinguish an existing status, as defined for instance by kinship, and create a new status, as defined by political and ritual domains of action. And what I am concerned with is the ethnographic fact that this is accompanied by the imposition of distinctive imperatives of apparel, speech, conduct and observance.

Tallensi say that eminent office, be it no more than the headship of a lineage, brings advantages of prestige and authority, and even some economic gains. These make office sought after. Yet they never tire of pointing out that such offices also carry heavy responsibilities, on the one hand to the living, but more onerously to the ancestors whose

[1] Recent references are given in Richards (1960).
[2] Details are given in Fortes (1949a).

place a chief or a lineage head now occupies. And the burdens of office are peculiarly symbolized, in their minds, by the taboos of office.

This is brought home to a newly elected chief or Earth-priest when he is installed. In the culminating rites he is secluded alone with the shrines of the lineage ancestors and the Earth, and it is believed that if he is not accepted by the ancestors he will not survive the ordeal.

The paramount duty of eminent office, Tallensi say, is to 'take care of' the country, that is, to maintain peace, and 'prosper' the people. This includes technical, jural and political tasks like arbitrating in disputes, representing the lineage and the clan in external affairs, and supervising communal undertakings. But secular authority and leadership are not enough or even fundamental. What matters most is the due performance of ritual obligations. That is why office holders have to be constantly vigilant in consulting diviners and bringing the right offerings to ancestors. In parenthesis, and bearing in mind what was earlier said about succession, it is worth adding that one of the major responsibilities of the head of a family or lineage is defined in similar terms with respect to his dependants in the domestic group.

But such private vigilance, left to the behests of conscience, is not, it seems, sufficient. Society, which confers office, demands that its proper exercise should be publicly accounted for. Tallensi recognize quite bluntly that this is necessary in part because men are fallible and prone to fall short of ideals. 'Who fears death', they say, 'until it is upon you?' But they also explain that accountability is part of the 'work' of office—that it is, in our language, a necessary feature of the tissue of rights and duties, authority and responsibility, which binds and incorporates office into society.

This accountability is ensured in a number of ways. In some societies it is built into the structure of political and ritual authority by being vested in countervailing office. This is the other side of 'king-makers' and electors. As hereditary councillors, or ritual functionaries, or custodians of sacred relics or myths or insignia that participate in the chiefship, they constitute a powerful disciplinary force to hold their ruler to his commitments, and friction between the parties is a not uncommon concomitant of the relationship. Indeed Dr. Richards, in her latest summary of one of the more elaborate constitutional arrangements of this type found in Africa, that of the Bemba, implies that some degree of friction may be inevitable and even necessary for the *bakabilo* to be able to keep control over the paramount chief.[1]

The Tallensi achieve a similar end, in the context of their more diffused political order, through the Cycle of the Great Festivals,[2] which lasts almost the whole dry season. The cycle begins with the celebration of the end of the rains, goes on to a sequence of harvest rites, and ends with ceremonies that foreshadow and hail the sowing season. But what is here relevant is that these ceremonies are the joint responsibility of all the politico-ritual lineage and clan heads of the country. They are so concatenated that every ceremony is either the necessary preliminary to another, or the essential conclusion of another; and each such leg of a sequence is the responsibility of a different office holder, acting in his capacity as the jural and ritual representative of his clan and lineage.

[1] Richards (1960).

[2] See references in Fortes (1945). Similar annual public ceremonies are widespread in West Africa and play the same part in politico-ritual relations. Cf. the Ashanti *Adae* and *Odwira* ceremonies described by Rattray (1927), Ch. XII, and the first-fruit rites of the Yakö (Forde, (1949)).

The prayers spoken in these ceremonies and the mimetic rituals employed have all the marks of the purely magical. In one rite, for example, the assembly of Earth-priests perambulates a sacred spot chanting invocations for good crops and solemnly miming the planting of grain. But the magic is really a secondary element. Such rites are bound to be about conspicuous common concerns, and crops are such a concern. There can be no general well-being without good crops in a precarious subsistence economy. But the magic cannot be mobilized without the support of the ancestors and the Earth; and this requires the ceremonial collaboration of all the officiants. Personal animosities may and do rage among them, for the clans of the Tallensi are jealously separatist and their heads compete for recognition. But they must collaborate or else they will anger the ancestors and the Earth, and so incur disaster for themselves as well as for the whole community.

The pattern of collaboration is easily seen. It consists in dramatizing salient episodes in the myths of the founding ancestors, and, what comes to the same thing, re-enacting key episodes in the installation ceremonies of the main officiants. So the ceremonial cycle confirms, annually, the occupation of each office and thus re-imposes on its holder his duties and capacities. This is quite explicit: the ceremonies are conducted in an idiom that highlights the ritual equality and indispensability of all the offices. All are equally essential. Each officiant can claim that his office and his ritual performances form the hub of the whole cycle and, consequently, the fount of tribal well-being.

Brief illustration must suffice. The cycle begins with a rite of terminating the rainy season on the day after the new moon of the first month of the dry season is seen. This rite is performed by the Bade Earth-priest, who sends messengers to inform neighbouring lineage heads when he has finished.

Immediately, the senior Chief of the area ceremonially brings out his ancestral clan drum, which only leaves its sanctuary on such special occasions. The series is now set in motion and the other office holders follow one after the other, each with his own rites and sacra. If there have been disputes between any of them, or their clans, the party which feels aggrieved will threaten to hold up everything until amends are made, and this sanction is always effective. The ceremonies cannot go on if there are unresolved quarrels between clans so they serve, incidentally, to reinforce peaceful relationships. In fact, there is an obligatory truce, phrased as a taboo on quarrelling in any form between clans and lineages, throughout the country during the cycle. As a consequence, marriages, which are the main source of disputes and quarrels between clans, are prohibited during its culminating and most critical stages.

We can see how the Festival Cycle serves as a ritually enforced check on the due discharge of their duties by Chiefs and Earth-priests. But to understand why this works we must examine the ritual itself more closely. I have time to describe only one of the simplest yet most solemn of the rites. It is, in effect, a dramatic recapitulation of the first arrival of the founding ancestor of the chiefly clans and his reception by the aboriginal Earth-priests. It takes place at night, at a sacred spot believed to be the site where these founding ancestors of the two groups first lived side by side in mutual amity. On this night no-one, except those actually taking part in the ritual, is allowed out of doors. The senior Chief, as the living representative of his first ancestor, dressed in the full regalia of his office—his red hat, his rich tunic, his sandals, and his amulets—and carrying his staff of office, goes in silent procession, followed by the elders of the lineages of the clan, to the sacred site. There he and his entourage take their seats on the rock which is supposed to have been the traditional seat of the founding ancestor and his elders. Presently the senior Earth-priest arrives with his clan elders. He is also accoutred in the prescribed costume of his office, that is, antelope skins, a black string cap and official amulets, and he carries a guinea corn stalk of a variety which only Earth-priests may carry about. In the black silence, he and his followers take their seats on another rock, equally sanctified by the myth as the original seat of *their* founding ancestor.

The parties cannot see one another, for fire and light are strictly forbidden. Minutes pass in silence. Then the Earth-priest calls out, 'Speak'. An elder of the chief, in tones of profound respect, announces that the chief has come to greet the priest. Greetings are then gravely exchanged between the parties. A stranger would be bound to infer, from their manner and tone, that they had not set eyes on one another during the twelve months which have passed since they last met in this place—though, in fact, they live cheek by jowl and in daily contact. The priest asks if all the lineages of the chiefly clan are present, and if any of them is not represented he demands an explanation. This is important, since the ceremony is a reaffirmation of the original compact between the two clans, and its binding force is impaired if all branches of both clans do not participate. At this point beer and flour for the libation are handed by the chief's spokesman to the priest.

Now comes the most solemn moment. The priest begins his invocation. It is a lengthy, vivid, reverent and pious speech, addressed formally to the ancestors but in fact equally to the participants. The ancestors are adjured to attend and to receive the libation. They are exhorted to bless and prosper the people and the country so that he, the priest, and his colleague the chief, may have everlasting renown. But the principal theme of the speech is a recitation of the

77

myth which, in Malinowski's words, constitutes the charter of the rite. At length the priest pours the libation and the dish is passed round for all those who are present to partake of it and so register their pledge of renewed amity. Parting salutations follow with mutual benedictions for good crops, good health for the people, and blessings on one another. Then the two parties file away in deep silence to their respective homes. When I had the privilege of attending this ceremony, which no stranger before or, I am sure, since, has seen, I came away filled with awe. But what is most significant about it is that it repeats one of the culminating rites performed by the Earth-priest at the installation of a new chief. Thus it is not only a dramatization of the myth of the origin of the politico-ritual relations of the two clan groups; it is also a rite of renewal of the chief's office.

*   *   *

The mesh of ritual collaboration, then, and the rites themselves, ensure that each office holder is accountable to his ancestors, to all his confrères, and through them to their clans. Furthermore, when each office holder is, in these ceremonies, reconfirmed in his office, he is graphically reminded that he holds it as a sacred trust granted to him on one side as the successor and perpetuator of the ancestors who founded the office and on the other as the representative of the clan in which the office is perpetually vested.

But let us return now to the taboos of office and ask again what their meaning is. Is it just a question of magical precautions inspired by insecurity and couched in terms of pre-logical thought? Can they be explained by the theory of divine kingship according to which it is all a matter of a magical association between the vigour and fertility of the ruler and the well-being and fertility of his people?

Light is thrown on the problem if we consider what happens among the Tallensi when a man borrows land for farming. Normally, land is loaned for farming only to a person who is related by kinship to the owner.[1] In accordance with this practice, a friend of mine asked a distant maternal kinsman to lend him a plot of land for an unspecified term of years. It turned out to be part of the patrimonial estate of the lineage to which the man who farmed it belonged. So he had to have the consent of all his male lineage kin before agreeing to the loan.

From our point of view, of course, borrowing or leasing land for farming is a purely economic and legal transaction of a technical order. Not so for the Tallensi. Patrimonial property is defined as property held in trust by each generation for posterity. It must, therefore, be accounted for to the ancestors, and misuse of it incurs mystical penalties. This means that the ancestors must be informed whenever a change is made in the tenancy of such property, and they must be asked to bless the transaction. Hence the message advising the would-be borrower that consent had been given for the loan of the land to him also desired him to bring fowls and guinea fowls to the lenders' home for the necessary sacrifices to the lenders' lineage ancestors.

The sacrifices were duly performed in the presence not only of the elders of the lenders' lineage but also of senior members of the borrower's lineage, who were thus tacitly implicated as witnesses of the arrangement. Tallensi explain that it is precisely this ritual act which transfers the right to use the land to the borrower, while at the same time making it clear that it is only a loan and that he will get no profit from using it unless he keeps in the good graces of the ancestors of the lender's lineage. They are, of course, also his own ancestors on his mother's side. This is important for

[1] See Fortes (1949a) for further details of such transactions.

a man has no ritual access to or claims upon ancestors who are outside his own genealogy.

But this was not the end of the formalities. Next day a meeting took place, on the land in question, between borrower and lender, each accompanied by senior and junior members of his lineage. Followed by the whole party, the lender first marched the borrower round the boundaries of the land. Rationally speaking this was superfluous, for they were known to all; but it is an essential feature of all such jural transactions among the Tallensi—as, indeed, in most African societies—that the subject-matter of any agreement shall be exhibited for all who are concerned to witness and approve; it must not be assumed to be known. This is a necessary safeguard in a culture which has no means of making written or other records.

The party now gathered in one corner of the land. Quite informally, the lender took up his hoe and cleared a small patch. As he finished, the two sons of the borrower took over and continued the hoeing for a short space. Having thus physically, as well as ceremonially and jurally, handed over the cultivation of the land to the borrower, the lender made a little speech: 'It is yours now to farm,' he said. 'The blessings of the ancestors will be with you. May no illness or misfortune ever harm you while you farm this land. Only prosperity will come to you from it.'

And now followed an action which specially interested me. The lender took a small dish of flour which the borrower had brought, scooped up a handful of soil from where he had just hoed, and mixed it well with the flour. He then licked some of the mixture and handed the dish to the borrower, who followed suit. Characteristically for the Tallensi, the latter called his sons to do so too. But at this point one of his own elders intervened. 'No, no,' he said, 'it is no affair of the boys or of anybody else. It is your affair only. You alone are responsible for the land and you alone are now bound by the taboos which anyone who starts a new farm has to observe.' The borrower nodded. He knew that he was now ritually prohibited from taking a new wife, attending funerals, hunting, and other common activities for a year from the time of the symbolical cutting of the first sod on his new farm. In addition, though a borrower never pays rent for land acquired in this manner, he is under a moral obligation to make a gift of grain grown on the land every year to the land-owner, who will use some of it to make a thanks-offering to his ancestors.

It would take me too far afield to spell out all the implications of this item, for every significant principle of Tale social structure and religious thought is encapsulated in it. What I want to draw attention to is only its relevance for my main theme. It shows us how religious ideas or rites are used to create a jural relationship between a person and property and so to place a technical fact within the moral order. And what is most striking is the parallel with the induction of an office holder into this office. For a would-be borrower of land is evidently turned into a tenant by a procedure of endowing him with a new element of ritual status in relation to the lineage and the ancestors of the land-owner. This creates rights in the land, but also consequential obligations to the owners. Now these obligations are not enforceable by material sanctions. They are only morally binding. But the efficacy of the moral bond is assured in no uncertain terms. The tenant and the owner bind themselves to mutual accountability and trust by symbolically taking into themselves the land which is the link between them and their joint concern, in the rite of eating of the soil.[1] And this

---

[1] The sanctity of this rite is enhanced by the belief that an oath which is peculiarly binding is one that is sworn by the Earth. This oath is sworn by touching the Earth with a wet finger and licking the finger.

is further symbolized in the personal taboos which the
tenant has to observe until he reaps his first harvest and so
gets established in his status as occupier of the land. On the
face of it these taboos have a magical intent, derived from
Tale mystical notions. For Tallensi see a parallel between
marrying a new wife and cultivating a new farm. Each
requires a man's undivided attention. To mix them up is to
risk conflicts of conscience and the anger of the ancestors;
for one cannot serve them single-mindedly if one's mind is
divided. Again, Tallensi believe that there is a dangerous
antithesis between everything associated with death and
everything associated with birth and new life, both among
men and with crops and herds. But a little thought soon
shows the true import of these taboos. It lies in their utility as
a tangible embodiment of, and a daily discipline for, the
moral obligations of tenancy.

The need for such a device is obvious if we consider how
difficult it is to visualize and adhere to moral obligations in
general or, for that matter, even in a particular context.
Taboos are a medium for giving tangible substance to
moral obligations. More than that, they are a means of keeping the feeling of moral obligation active all the time, so that
whenever occasion arises to translate the duty into performance we are in a state of readiness for that. If an athlete does
not keep fit by means of self-appropriated food, exercise and
sleep taboos he will fail when it comes to the real test. And
what is more, taboos refer to observable behaviour. So they
serve as a means by which a person can account to himself, as
well as to the world at large, for the conscientious discharge
of his moral obligations.

It is easy to see how this analysis applies to politico-ritual
functionaries. For them, too, their taboos symbolize to
themselves and to the world at large their endowment by
society with the parts they have to play—their licences, as

Hughes puts it, to hold office. But more than that, they symbolize their appropriation of these parts, to return to the formula which I used earlier. Since adherence to them is in part a public act, the taboos also validate their incorporation into the social structure in their status as holders of office. Looking back on the brief account I have given of the religious context of their tasks, duties and social relations, we can see how their taboos have the same symbolical value in holding them to their moral commitment to their parts as do those of a borrower of land. It is not magic of the 'divine kingship' kind that imposes ritual forms on these offices. Their religious character is a way of investing with binding force the moral obligations to society, for its well-being and prosperity, which those who accept office must solicitously translate into actions.

*   *   *

It has long been understood that religious conceptions and ritual institutions fulfil critical integrative functions in primitive societies. Malinowski once spoke of them as 'the cement of the social fabric'. But what I have tried to examine is something more specific. If we look behind the networks and hierarchies of social relations to the persons whose conduct and activities make up the working of a social structure, we see that every part played in the stream of process is made up of diverse components. There are always economic components, in that goods and services of some kind or another are used up and produced, and there are invariably jural components, since roles are exercised as a matter of right and duty, subject to rules and sanctions of a juridical order. What I wish to stress is that there is also invariably a moral component. This represents the mutual commitment to his roles of person and society focused in status and office. Just as society expresses its commitment to the individual when it invests him with office, so he must feel committed to his roles, statuses and offices if he is to fulfil their requirements adequately. To paraphrase Redfield, I see religious prescriptions as serving to symbolize and focus this moral component.[1]

Does this analysis apply to every kind of status or is it limited to eminent office and to special categories of social and economic relations of the kind we would call contractual? A test case will come to the mind of every anthropologist. Among the Tallensi every person is ostensibly by right of birth a member of his patrilineal clan and lineage. From this irreducible fact of what Linton called 'ascribed' status flow numerous attributes of jural, economic and ritual status. They include eligibility for politico-ritual office, rights of inheritance and succession, the privileges and duties of cult allegiance and other elements of citizenship. The individual has no choice; he is bound by the chances of birth. Is there a parallel with office here?

Tale custom is conveniently explicit on this point.[2] A person has membership in his lineage by right of birth only if he is his father's legitimate child. Thus it is not the mere fact of birth but legitimate birth that is decisive; and legitimacy derives from the jural rights over his wife's reproductive powers conferred on a person's father in return for the bride price. It is because a man is invested with (licensed for) husbandhood that his children are able to be born into their 'ascribed' status. And, as might be expected, a religious hallmark is added. It is a strict rule that a child must be born under its father's roof. If a woman bears a child elsewhere than in her marital home, particularly in her

---

[1] See Forde (1957), p. 11, for an illuminating comment on similar ideas among the Yakö.

[2] I here summarize data given more fully in Fortes (1949a), but I failed, there, to appreciate the significance I now see in these facts.

father's place, it is a ritual pollution and a cleansing rite must be performed. Obviously this is an assertion, in the idiom of taboo, of the jural disjunction between a woman's status as daughter and her status as wife and mother, and the consequential differentiation of matrilateral filiation from patrilineal descent. But it is also an assertion of the father's right to incorporate his offspring in his lineage. Tallensi explain the custom by reference to the ancestor cult. A person must be born under the aegis of his patrilineal ancestors, since it is upon them that he will be dependent for the ordering of his life. Indeed a person is not incorporated into his natal lineage until his father has ascertained through a diviner which of his ancestors wishes to be his spirit guardian.

There is much more to be said on this subject, notably by adducing the contrast of the illegitimate child. But I think my point is clear. The fact of birth is only a necessary, not a sufficient, condition for kinship and descent status. There is a procedure for establishing this status as a relationship with society and the ancestors; and it is focused in ritual symbolism and observance. Analogous customs are found in other African societies. In Ashanti, for example, an infant is not deemed to be human until it has lived to the eighth day, when it is named and thus incorporated into its family and lineage.[1]

This is not the only way in which religious concepts and customs are utilized to mark status acquired by birth and thus to focus the moral commitments entailed by it. Tale totemic beliefs and avoidances, by reference to which separate clans and lineages are distinguished from one another, are obligatory by virtue of descent and kinship status.

---

[1] See Rattray (1927), Ch. VI. It is worth noting that both Fustel de Coulanges (1864), Ch. VIII, and Van Gennep (*op. cit.*, p. 101) perceived what I am here restating.

Like similar observances in other tribal societies, they have no obvious rational basis. What, for instance, can be the economic sense of a taboo on eating a fairly rare variety of grasshopper, or the utility of forbidding all first-born children from eating the domestic fowl? Their purpose is purely symbolical in the same way as are taboos that identify office. They are a constant reminder of the norms and commitments a person is bound to as a member of his lineage and clan. They stand for the inalienable bonds with the ancestors and with living kin.

The burden of my thesis is that societies distinguish between the individual and his offices, statuses or roles. It is because the individual is more than the offices or statuses or roles he may have, because he stands over against them, that ritual is needed in order to confer them upon him, or, alternatively, to deprive him of them. In this way office is entrusted to the holder in a binding manner, or again, conversely, legitimately stripped from him. Ritual presents office to the individual as the creation and possession of society or a part of society into which he is to be incorporated through the office. Ritual mobilizes incontrovertible authority behind the granting of office and status and thus guarantees its legitimacy and imposes accountability for its proper exercise.

This raises a complex problem. If there is such a dialectical relationship between individual and office, we must expect to find some degree of conceptual awareness, or at least of institutional recognition of the uniqueness, the individuality, as it were, of the individual in all societies. I believe this to be the case, paradoxical as it may seem. As I have shown elsewhere, the Tallensi, like other peoples of West Africa, give cultural recognition to this fact in their concept of Fate.[1] Religious concepts and values are used to assign in-

[1] See Fortes (1959).

dividuality to the individual so that he may be able to take on diverse roles, statuses and offices in order to play his part in society.

Robert Redfield, whom I have quoted several times, speaking of early city-states remarks (*op. cit.*, p. 65) that religion becomes to them a 'way of making citizens'. Citizenship, surely, means the sum total of all the legitimate offices, statuses and roles a person can have in his society. In this sense Redfield's dictum sums up pithily the theme of my paper, and suggests what must be added to Van Gennep's model in order to explain why ritual is indispensable in *rites de passage*.

What I have in mind can be exemplified by reference to initiation ceremonies. In terms of Van Gennep's model they are the means of marking and organizing the transition from childhood to socially recognized adulthood. Restated in terms of the model I am proposing they are the means of divesting a person of his status as a child in the domestic domain and of investing him with the status of actual or potential citizen in the politico-jural domain.[1] Ordeals and mutilations are more than conspicuous ways of emphasizing entry into the new status. The right to exercise adult sexuality, that is sexuality in marriage for procreative purposes, as opposed to childish sexuality, is one of the distinctive prerogatives and responsibilities of citizenship. One purpose of initiation rites, and, for that matter, the main purpose of female initiation, is to confer this right and to do this in such a way that the commitments implied in its acquisition are accepted as a necessary moral and jural concomitant of citizenship. I believe that this reformulation assists in comprehending the need for ritual in such ceremonies.

[1] See Fortes in Goody (Ed.), 1958, *No. 1, loc. cit.*

Postscript

This essay had gone to press when Professor Roman Jakobson drew my attention to Professor Ernst H. Kantorowicz's profound and erudite book, *The King's Two Bodies*. It is, in Dr. Kantorowicz's own words, a history of 'corporational modes of thinking' concerning the connection between the king's 'Body natural' as a mortal man and his 'Body politic' as an immortal office, to re-phrase the celebrated formula in Plowden's 'Reports' of the mid-sixteenth century. Dr. Kantorowicz casts his net wider than did his illustrious predecessor, F. W. Maitland, and thus illuminates aspects of the problem that are of particular interest to an anthropologist. Dr. Kantorowicz's elucidation of the notion that 'the king never dies' in mediaeval political theory and theological doctrine, notably in England, is pregnant with matter for thought for an anthropologist concerned with the theme of my present essay. One cannot fail to be impressed by the acute understanding mediaeval jurists displayed of the sociological realities at issue in the question of succession to kingship.

My essay, limited as it is in its scope, would have been enriched in several places if I had had the stimulus of this book at the time I wrote it.

DEATH AND SUCCESSION
an analysis of Yakö mortuary ceremonial
by DARYLL FORDE

Introduction

COMPLEX and protracted mortuary ceremonies follow the deaths of senior men among the Yakö of Eastern Nigeria. They involve the provision of gifts, feasts and payments over a wide range of persons and groups. It has been a common-place since the pioneer studies of Van Gennep, Radcliffe-Brown and Malinowski that the main social significance of such ceremonies, including the provision and transfers of goods and the changes of status associated with them, was to be found in a reaffirmation of the solidarity and a restoration of the structure of social groups that had suffered loss. These ritual responses and social restorations have, however, been mainly studied and interpreted with reference to the groups of kin affected by a death. Funerary ritual in primitive societies has, accordingly, been largely seen as a manifestation of the importance of kinship as a mode of social grouping and succession in such societies.

Yakö mortuary ceremonial might, at first sight, appear to be anomalous in this respect or even to discredit such generalization. For while significant social recognitions and readjustments take place within kin groups following death, these do not receive elaborate ritual expression or major emphasis. And although there is also symbolic expression of condolence between groups of kin concerned, the most prominent relations of the bereaved kin, and the ceremonial and practical activities that these entail, are with external groups to which the dead man belonged and to which his kin are called upon to fulfil obligations.

This apparent divergence in form and emphasis from those more commonly discussed may, however, as I shall attempt to show, be accounted for by the strong development among the Yakö of organized social relations outside the sphere of kinship. These have been especially developed in a number of associations in which the mutual interests and the maintenance of the prestige of their members are combined with the exercise of ritual and secular power in the community.

The influence of these associations has, it would appear, become so important in defining social roles and relations that the ritual and economic emphasis on solidarity and social replacement at death has been largely concentrated on them. Kinship relations have accordingly become most significant with reference to rights and obligations to the associations, rather than an autonomous field within which social readjustment and its ritual expression take place. Yakö mortuary ceremonies and the transfers of goods at death thus afford an index of the status of the associations in Yakö society. For, as will be shown, they both symbolize and reinforce their dominance in social control and prestige in the village community.

Some Features of Yakö Social Structure

The Yakö are a yam-growing and palm-oil-producing people living in forest country immediately east of the middle Cross River in Eastern Nigeria. They live in large compact villages each of which controls a surrounding tract of country and within which territorial divisions or wards and their component patrikin exercise more specific rights to land and the exploitation of resources. The largest village of Umor, which had a population of over 11,000 in the late thirties, consists of four wards each occupied by a number of localized patriclans. These patriclans, ranging in size from about 50 to 200 adult men, are composed of a number of lineages of 15 to 30 men within which common descent by birth or adoption is usually traced and emphasized. Kinship between the lineages, while a postulate for solidarity, is often fictive and untraced. The patriclans within a ward do not claim and are not united on a basis of common descent and although the governing association of a ward—the Yakamben—includes members from all patriclans, this traditional organization is not an assembly of clan heads or representatives. Subject to the collective rights and authority of a ward over its recognized territory, each patriclan controls and defends occupation of its own dwelling area in the village and of tracts of land in which men establish, and inherit within their lineages, rights to farm plots and clusters of oil palms and other valuable trees.[1]

But rights to stores of wealth are inherited matrilineally among the Yakö. A close matrilineal relative, known as the Burier of the Matrikin (Lejima Obonganen), takes charge of a person's money, harvest of yams, livestock, cloth and other moveable goods at death. But he is in part dependent on the goodwill and co-operation of a corresponding relative selected by the patrikin from among themselves, the Kepun Obonganen. And the latter can also ensure that appropriate contributions are made from the dead relative's wealth towards the feast, gifts and payments for which he is responsible on behalf of the patrikin during the obsequies.

The disposition of the remaining property is supervised by the elders of the matrilineage, a body of kin comparable in scale to the patrilineage of twenty or so adult men within which succession to house sites, land and trees is exercised. During their lives men expect to receive and give pecuniary help in situations of personal need and obligation within

[1] See Forde (1937); (1938); (1950).

their matrilineage. They receive most of the payments made for marriages to their sister's daughters, the women of the matrilineage, and are responsible for any repayments on divorce.[1]

The matrilineages are themselves parts of larger matriclans of which the former are regarded as segments formed in the course of their growth. The matriclans are important ritual units for the fertility of their women and collectively for the prosperity of the whole community. For each matriclan is associated with one of the Fertility Spirit shrines (Ase) whose priests (Bi'ina) form the core of a village council of priests responsible for periodic village rituals at which peace and prosperity are sought. This council controls the selection from the appropriate matriclan of the successors to the priesthoods of these spirits as well as those of other village cults. Traditionally it also directed the secular government of the community as a whole, as the authority for the observance of custom and for judgment in serious offences and major disputes.

While the Yakö themselves were not interested until recently in travelling abroad to trade, their economy has not been self-contained. With the surpluses of their production of yams, palm oil, dwarf cattle and other supplies, they have over several generations obtained goods brought by traders from the Cross River and beyond it to the west. They have also been intermediaries in the trading of guns and powder for supplies of bush meat and camwood from the forest peoples to the east. The returns from these exchanges could be accumulated, formerly in the old currency of iron bars and brass rods and more recently in West African coinage. This wealth has provided a means of engaging in further transactions which could enhance the prestige of an indi-

[1] See Forde (1941); 'Double Descent among the Yakö', in Radcliffe-Brown and Forde (Eds.) (1950).

vidual and of his kin among whom he could gain a corresponding influence. Wealth has also enabled a man to take several wives early in life, thereby increasing the size of his farming unit and yam harvest as well as enjoying the prestige of a large household. Some resources were also formerly expended on the purchase of children brought mainly by Ibo traders from the east. The Yakö treated such children, who were known as yafoli, as adopted junior members of both the patrikin and matrikin of their purchasers who gained prestige and influence both for themselves and for their kin groups, whose numbers they increased.

But the successful accumulation of wealth by individuals, in the various forms of large yam harvests, currency, livestock and yafoli, has not only been a means of gaining prestige and securing a following within their patrilineal and matrilineal kin-groups. It has also been used to compete for status and influence in the ward and the village. And such influence and competition have been mainly achieved within the framework of various associations.

The Associations

Apart from the village council of priests, the Yabot, and the village corporation of Diviners, the Yabunga, both of which had some of the characteristics of self-perpetuating associations, there were in Umor in the thirties eight other men's associations to which membership was usually open through succession to a kinsman at his death. The provision of mortuary feasts for these associations as well as admission payments for suitable successors was, at the same time, obligatory on the close kinsmen of the dead member. These in turn had a claim on his wealth to meet such payments and to provide the association with animals, palm wine and other provisions for it to hold the feasts at which the former member was honoured and the new one admitted.[1]

The sphere of activity of three of these associations extended over the village as a whole and their members were drawn from all the wards. These were Ikpungkara, Okengka and Okundum. Ikpungkara was particularly prominent on account both of the large payments demanded for admission and of its political power in the village. Its members, who numbered about forty, formed a close-knit group and were pledged to secrecy by the supernatural sanctions of their spirit cult. Its explicit authority concerned the settlement of frequent disputes, between individuals and lineages of different clans and wards, over rights to farm land and the detection and punishment of thefts of cows. Cows were very valuable, being worth about one hundred brass rods, but they had to be left free to browse in the vicinity of the village and were accordingly liable to be stolen surreptitiously for disposal to strangers. But Ikpungkara had also gained a general ascendancy which made it influential in all village affairs. It intervened, with the approval of the Yabot (council of priests), in any major issue where the detection and punishment of offenders or the determination of rights were difficult.

Some village priests became members of Ikpungkara by virtue of their offices but admission was otherwise obtained by patrilineal succession to a deceased member. In either case succession was both a right and an obligation. It was, on the

[1] Membership in the Village Priests Council follows from appointment to specific ritual offices, hence no question of payments by kinsfolk for compulsory succession or the provision of memorial feasts arises. The position is similar, in a more limited field, for the corporation of Diviners, see Forde (1958). While most of the payments in the thirties were being made in Nigerian currency, they and the value of supplies provided for the feasts were still reckoned in brass rods, the conventional exchange rate for which was sixpence per rod.

one hand, of considerable advantage to a kin group to have a member in Ikpungkara both for prestige and in case of involvement in serious disputes. On the other hand the association itself was able to enforce the presentation of an acceptable successor and oblige his kin to provide feasts and gifts to it as well as admission fees valued at over 400 rods. For failure or undue delay, livestock of the group concerned would be raided and a fine thus imposed.

Okundum, the name of which may be translated literally as 'body (or association) of men' (kokum—group, odum—man), was said to be an older association, also known as Itumö, that had been overshadowed by Ikpungkara in more recent times with regard to the settlement of disputes in the village as a whole. But it continued to offer both magical protection against, and enquiry into, trespass on farms and the stealing of crops from them. Its establishment was traditionally associated with one of the matriclan shrines which had sanctioned it, and its head was selected from certain of the patriclans in the ward where this shrine was situated. On the death of a member it also demanded a feast and payments for a successor.

Okengka, the village cult group which controlled the sanctions of a leopard spirit for certain ritual offences and for infractions of its judgments, especially on disputes between different wards, drew its membership from the associations of Leaders in the various wards (the Yakamben) whose authority they united and reinforced.

Membership in Okengka did not necessarily follow by succession among the patrikin of a deceased member. But on the other hand a new member was usually admitted only when one died, the feast in his honour being the occasion for this, and the patriclan of the member who had died had a strong claim to the admission of one of its other Yakamben to the Okengka group. The kin of the deceased member had in any case an obligation to provide for the feast. If another Okamben from that patriclan wished to join he and the elders could demand a portion of the deceased member's wealth as a contribution to the payments in money, goats and a cow valued in all at 140 rods which had to be provided at admission.

The other five associations were organized within the wards, so that there were parallel and independent associations of the same name and character in each ward.[1]

The Yakamben—the Leaders of the Ward—not only conducted periodical initiations of the boys of the ward and a rite after farms were cleared each year, but also constituted the governing and judicial body for the ward, giving judgment between people of different patriclans and directing the public obligations of the age-sets. Membership was increasing considerably in the thirties but earlier there had been only some thirty members in each ward. They included some men from each patriclan who were usually but not necessarily from different lineages within it. Priestheads of patriclans and matriclan priests resident in the ward were expected to become members. The patrilineages and clans both valued membership by their men on the one hand, and on the other were under an obligation to provide an acceptable successor to a member from their group at his death. The mortuary feast and the payments for admission were valued at 200–300 brass rods. The patrikin of a member who died could, with the support of the Yakamben, demand a part of his property to provide for these.

The leadership of the Yakamben was also subject to rules of succession with the provision of feasts and payments. In each ward two or three patriclans laid claims to succession to the position of Ogbolia (the head) and of Ogometu (his deputy). These were clans within which, they claimed, the

[1] See Forde (1950), 'Ward Organization'.

offices had been held in the past and they sought to exercise their rights in rotation. Within them particular lineages might also claim priority in providing successors on the ground that men of their lineage had held these offices in previous generations. There had sometimes been keen, even bitter, rivalry for these offices between candidates and their followers from different clans and lineages. But one essential condition for securing them had been generosity in feasts to the Yakamben at the death of previous leaders, and substantial payments on succession.

Within the larger membership there was an inner and directing group of about a dozen men who had the custody of the cult objects—a spirit bundle, known as Ekpa, and the Okowa, two fringed masks surmounted by skulls, which embodied spirits that sanctioned the Ligwomi cult, the initiation of boys into membership of the male community of the ward, and which were also invoked at an annual prosperity rite—Kekpan—in the ward square. Membership of this group was also expected to pass at death to an Okamben from the same patriclan which became responsible for further payments to the value of 100 rods and a feast at his admission.

Thus ritual and secular authority in the wards lay not with a body of kinsmen nor with representatives of kin-groups as such, but with an association of those who had sufficient standing in the ward as well as backing from their patrikin and the wealth needed for admission. On the other hand, as we shall see, this association could, during the funeral ceremonies for a deceased member, effectively demand that his kin should present an acceptable successor and provide the fees for his admission. It was thus able to maintain its membership, together with a flow of feasts and payments, and also to assert its prestige and authority in relation to the patriclans of the ward.

97

Ebiabu was a graded association in which all boys of the ward, excluding yafoli, were admitted to the lower grades for a small payment. But large payments and obligatory succession applied to the senior grades, which arranged and carried out punitive action against recalcitrant offenders in the ward, subject in principle, if not always in practice, to authorization by the Ogbolia of the Yakamben. The name (meaning Ghost-Dogs) and some features of this association were derived from the Agwa'aguna to the south.

Ebiabu initiations were usually held during the period of funeral ceremonies of members of the senior grades. The patrikin of a senior grade member who died were required to give goats and wine for a feast which was augmented or prolonged by the initiation payments. Most small boys joined its first grade (Abuodum) for which their fathers paid a small fee of five rods to a senior grade. This entitled them to join in the public assemblies, processions and songs of Ebiabu. The second grade, Ebiabu proper, which young men could join after marriage, required a payment of 20 rods together with a goat, yams and salt. If the father or a matrikinsman, who had been expected to provide all or part of the fee of a young man ready to join, died, Ebiabu itself would support a claim from the Buriers.

Admission to the third grade (Abu) which included about a third of the adult men of a ward, required another payment of 100 or more rods and a cow, together with large quantities of palm wine and yams, sufficient in fact to feed all the members. Here again a younger man who had not yet entered this grade had a right to claim a substantial part of the fee from his father's wealth if he died.

But Ebiabu activities were directed by a smaller group of about half a dozen men, the Imiedong (Inside the House), who were usually Yakamben (Leaders of the Ward). They could invite more senior and approved Abu to join them and these were then expected to make them a further money payment and provide a feast. The Imiedong co-operated with the Yakamben in securing the enforcement of the latter's judgments in the ward where necessary by calling on a body of Abu members to coerce recalcitrants. Spanning the different patriclans and age-sets as they did, an intervening force from the Abu members could be mustered and ordered out if disputes over their rights and obligations between men of different patriclans or age-sets in the ward threatened to become violent.

Of the other associations, Eblömbe—the Black Ones—had been a body of leading fighters that organized the defence of its ward against attack and led war parties on other settlements. While their activities had been in principle subject to the Village War Leaders, who belonged to the Village Council of Priests, and the Yakamben, the Eblömbe association appeared to have often enjoyed considerable freedom of action in the past. Membership was still coveted as a recognition of courage and also for participation in their elaborate dances that mimed the suspense and excitement of warfare. The kin of a member who died had to provide for a feast and could present a successor for whom payments, including the feast, were valued at 200 rods.

Ukwa or Obam had as its *raison d'être* the ambushing of victims in neighbouring areas to provide skulls and human flesh for the burial rites of the priests of village cults. Again, provision of a feast was obligatory on the kin of a member who died. Finally Kodjo, the association of hunters which maintained a hunting camp in the bush, organized hunts to provide game for some rituals and at the funerals of members whose kin had to provide for their feasts.[1]

[1] There was a further and quite influential association with a large membership in each ward which, although payments were required for membership, and a feast was usually given to it by the kin when a

Thus we see that most of these village and ward associations have been able to enforce succession and all of them to obtain feasts from the kin during the obsequies of their members. In the past they could bring cases before the Ogbolia, the head of the Leaders of the Ward, or to the Yabot, the priests' council of the village, against those who failed on the death of a member to provide for a mortuary feast and present a successor, together with the admission payments, during the period of the funeral ceremonies. When judgments in support of their claims had been given, direct action could be taken. Surprise visits to kill or carry off goats or cows would be made to the compounds of the men concerned either by the association itself or by Ebiabu in the ward or Ikpungkara in the village. By the thirties such cases had also been recognized in the Native Court for the district and defaulters could be sued for failure to provide 'funeral expenses'.

Whether it was seen as a right, an obligation or an opportunity, the succession to membership in these associations justified demands by the close patrikin and the elders of the patriclan for an appropriate portion of the wealth of the dead man as a contribution towards the payment for the new admission as well as for the obligatory feast. If the matrikin Burier, who had custody of the currency and without whose consent the livestock and yams could not be used, refused this contribution, the issue was formerly laid before the Ogbolia of the ward or the Yabot. A favourable judgment from them usually sufficed since they could authorize

---

member died, was not able to enforce succession. Known as Ngkpe, it controlled a Leopard and other spirits that protected its members against injustice and misbehaviour of women. The absence of any requirement of succession appeared to be connected with its general tendency to opposition to the Ward Leaders and the village council which refused to recognize it ritually or juridically. Men belonging to Ngkpe had to renounce it before they could join these (see Forde (1957)).

the seizing of livestock in the compounds of matrikinsmen if it were not accepted.

These associations all claimed to control spirits which protected their members and lent them prestige and influence. These powers were also, for several associations, extended to others for legitimate ends, and were mainly sought for the protection of property. The association had its sign, usually a bundle of leaves or plaited stems of a particular plant, which could, on payment of a fee by non-members, be attached to an animal, a tree or the entrance to a plot. This gave the association an interest in, and rights concerning, the property so protected. Its leaders could not only lay a complaint with the Ogbolia or the Yabot if rights were infringed, but sought also to discover the offender, and a favourable judgment included payment of a fine to the association as well as compensation to the owner. This capacity not only afforded the association a means of attaining prestige and influence, but provided its members with a flow of payments in fees and fines which were distributed from time to time or used for wine and food at their rituals and celebrations.[1]

[1] Some women's associations, although fewer and less influential, had analogous roles within the wards. Thus a ward association known as Ekoaso which carried out an initiation for girls regarded as similar to that of Ligwomi by the Yakamben, protected women's property and interests. With regard to the latter, it could resist actions by the Ward Leaders or meet failure to settle a protracted and disturbing dispute by threatening the evacuation of the ward by its women who would go temporarily to live with kinsfolk elsewhere. It also recruited its membership by enforced succession, requiring the matrikin of a member who died to provide the admission payment of a goat, a fowl and four rods, for a young married kinswoman living in the ward. There was also a women's association in each ward known as Oyongko which performed dances during the funerals of their members or their kin and of prominent men in the ward as well as at the end of the main phases of the farming year. Its dancers also visited to perform in other wards and villages on the basis of kinship ties between some of its members and persons being mourned or celebrated there. On all these occasions it expected gifts of food and small sums of money. Oyongko had a punitive spirit (Oyongko edet)

There were also some other men's associations within the ward in which there were no obligations of succession. These had no spirit cult. But if a member, or one of his close kin, died the members assembled to visit the compound and perform the songs and dances and effectively demand that supplies for a feast be given to them. Most of these associations were convivial and joined by younger men on their own account. But one, known as Epoli, was an association of rich men, osu, open to those who had established their reputation for wealth by the acquisition of one or more yafoli. To gain recognition in the village as a person of wealth, a man had to join Epoli. At his death Epoli commemorated his membership, and his heirs had to provide a substantial feast at which the celebration took place.

The Character of Yakö Mortuary Ceremonial

At the death of one of their members an association assembles in his compound during the obsequies. The leaders bid him farewell in terms which reflect their own importance as an organization. Its masked figures and sacred objects are displayed in a dance. His kinsmen are then asked to give the animals and other supplies for its feast.

A man's age-set also assembles at his death. A house is set aside for them during the obsequies in the compound where he lived. Here some of them sleep and the widows cook food for them.

Within the patriclans themselves there are also small ritual associations which have the custody of some of their mortuary insignia. These consist of an elephant-tusk trumpet (leniga), which is blown to announce a death, and of two

at whose pot shrine members were initiated and which was believed to give them protection. Since the majority of women living in a ward join by offering a goat at one of its seasonal dances, it served to express their *esprit de corps*. But it performed no rites of public concern and there was no compulsory succession to a deceased member.

decorated staves (yakpunun), kept by the Kekbun association, which are stamped on the grave at the burial and when
the grave is re-made at the end of the mortuary period.
These are brought from the patriclan assembly house,
where the slit-gong is beaten to announce the death to the
village, and are displayed in the dead man's compound
throughout the obsequies. Gifts must be made to Kekbun
by the matrikin and widows of the deceased in return for
their use. There is also a group known as Kuka which
demands a payment by the widows for their purification at
the end of the ceremonies.

Both the patriclans and the matriclans are associated with
tutelary spirits which are ritually invoked at their shrines for
the resolution of conflicts and the promotion of welfare
among those belonging or related to these two sets of
major kin-groups. The patriclan head (Obot Kepun) is the
priest of its spirit shrine (epundet) and as such also has the
secular role of seeking harmony and consensus within it.
The priests (Bi'ina) of the fertility spirits have similar roles
in relation to the matriclans from the senior of which they
are chosen. But, apart from rituals of succession to the office
of priest, neither of these spirits is invoked at the deaths of
members of the clans. Both patriclan and matriclan priestheads may be, and often are, concerned in secular questions
of succession and inheritance in which they should seek to
ensure that just and fitting arrangements are made. But they
perform no rituals for the dead at their shrines. Nor do the
clan members assemble as a body to manifest their bereave-
ment, to reaffirm their solidarity or to assign a future status
to the member who has died. The collective concern of the
patriclan finds ceremonial expression only in the drumming
of the gong in its assembly house and, with the consent of
the Kekbun group, the transfer of the mortuary staves and
the trumpet, which can be blown by any of the kinsmen,

from the assembly house to the dead man's compound. For the matriclan there is no ritual action on its own behalf.

The only ceremonies conducted by and for kin-groups are two feasts in which elders of the patriclan and of the matriclan successively and reciprocally provide a goat. After exchanges of declarations of concern and goodwill during the presentation of the goat, the two groups sit separately in the compound and a portion of the meat is carried from the providers to the others. While it is mainly the lineages concerned and not all the members of the clans that participate in these feasts, the presence of the Head of the patriclan with some of its elders and the presence of the Priest of the matriclan do make explicit the reciprocal concern and undertakings of the two larger groups.

Kinsfolk from both clans usually visit the compound individually and in considerable numbers to bid farewell to the dead man and make small gifts in condolence to his close kin during the mortuary period. But listings of visitors made during several mournings suggest that they may well be outnumbered by others, notably fellows in the age-sets and in associations to which the deceased and his close kinsmen belonged.

The Funeral of a Patriclan Head

The participation of associations in obsequies among the Yakö and the extent to which the custodians of the deceased's wealth, the two Buriers, and other kin are concerned in transactions with them, vary of course according to the social statuses that the deceased occupied. The position of women, which cannot be considered here, differs from that of men, since with the exception of one or two village ritual offices, they can participate only in their own more limited range of associations. Similarly, the death of a young man rarely involves action by, or succession in, the more important associations. And, while such a death is a source of grief and a cause of social reorientation in his household and among his close kin, it does not have repercussions on the larger kin groups or occasion rituals within them. The Kekbun staves, for example, are only brought out for elders.

The dominant part played by associations in mortuary ceremonial becomes apparent at the death of older men who have belonged to some of the main associations of the ward and village. This can be illustrated by a brief account of the ceremonies and transactions that followed the death of the priest-head of one patriclan in the thirties.

Oka, the Obot Kepun of a large patriclan in Egbisum ward, an old man of about 70 years, died one evening shortly after harvest after being seriously ill for a few days. His death, which had been expected, was announced at once by prolonged funereal drumming on the slit-gong in the patriclan assembly house. But, although as head of the patriclan he had performed many rites at the clan shrine, there was no ritual at this time. Oka had died on the first of the three days in the Yakö week of six days in which ceremonies concerning men must be held, and would be buried in his house on the third of these. During the night, the grave pit was dug in the house by some close patrikinsmen. His body was dressed in new clothes and ornaments. His face was whitened and he was seated near the doorway to receive farewells. In all this his widows and sons were assisted by one or two of his matrikinswomen, including his sister, who came at once to the compound. On the next day the Kekbun trumpet and staves were set out on a deerskin before his house. There they remained for six weeks while the various ceremonies were held and until his grave was re-made and his wealth was distributed. For their use, goats would have to be given by the matrikin and the widows of the dead man to provide feasts for the dozen members of Kekbun who ritually stamped down the grave with them.

Meanwhile a group of fifteen or more men, Oka's close patrikin and one or two men from most of the eight lineages of which the clan was composed, assembled in the house of the senior widow. There they received the condolences of individual visitors of whom many came throughout this and later days. But they were also there to consider the succession to the headship of the patrikin itself and other positions Oka held, and to decide on the patrikinsman who should be responsible for the burial on their behalf. For the patrikin Burier (Kepun Obonganen) does not merely take charge of activities in the compound, he is also the custodian of the rights and obligations of the dead man's patrikin and, as such, he has to negotiate with the similar Burier appointed by the matrikin.

Although they are approved or at least must be recognized by the elders concerned before they can act, the patrikin and matrikin Buriers are not thought of as representatives of these clans. Nor do they behave as such. They are normally close junior kinsmen of the deceased who have personal interests in the inheritance and successions arising from the death. The duty of the elders is to approve men whom they consider the most appropriate among the close kin concerned and to prevent quarrels among these over the choice. And here they are governed not simply by seniority or directness of descent, but also by expediency. The matrikin Burier becomes not only the custodian of the dead man's money and stock, he has a first claim on it himself after all the feasts and payments have been given and so has an interest in minimizing the outlays on these. Similarly, when allocating the distribution of the harvested yams he keeps as large a part as he decently can for himself. But this inheritance of money and goods carries with it obligations for later help to other and especially junior matrikin which may or may not be readily forthcoming. The elders of the matrilineage should therefore be concerned with the interests of the matrikin and with the good name of the lineage in meeting outside obligations. Their influence can be exercised by refusing to recognize one who does not reassure them and whom they consider neither worthy of trust for dealing fairly with his own kin nor capable of dealing correctly but shrewdly with other persons and groups—in particular with ward and village associations and successors to membership in them. The position is similar if weaker in the case of the patrikin Burier. He has to secure the means from his kinsmen, from the matrikin and from his own resources to meet obligations of hospitality during the ceremonies and to contribute towards payments for feasts and admissions to associations. This is, however, an opportunity for ensuring the admission of himself or someone of his choice. So that in the general interest of the patriclan it is important to select a man who is likely to behave well as he gains in status among his patrikin and who has himself the means to contribute substantially for the feasts and payments so that heavy demands are not made on other patrikin, and especially those of other lineages, to fulfil these obligations of hospitality and succession. The patriclan as a whole is concerned that its good name should be maintained and that it is not embroiled in disputes with the matrikin and the associations.

Early in the day following death, the elders of Oka's matrilineage, both men and women, arrived with the priest of the Atewa spirit of the Yakangkang matriclan of which the lineage was part. After the priest and others had addressed Oka in farewell, they came over to the patriclan elders and condoled with them. These thanked the matrikin but reminded them in a customary speech that on the patriclan fell the task of burying a member of their matriclan, of giving food and wine to those who came to condole, of satisfying those who would make demands on them, but that the wealth of their dead patrikinsman would duly be handed over to the Burier of the matrikin.

The spokesman of the matrikin declared their trust in them and agreed that the proper demands of others should be met. This meant in practice that the matrikin Burier should not dispute the appropriate portions of the wealth for those feasts, gifts and payments that would have to be given during the obsequies to meet obligations for which the patriclan would be responsible. The matrikin then gave the patrikin an ekpanpom, i.e. advance gift (epon) to the patriclan (kepun), a customary token offered in condolence by visiting groups, consisting of a brass rod, a clay pot and a floor mat. The house of Oka's second wife was given to them for their use during the obsequies. As was customary, a few older matrikinswomen lived there throughout the period while matrikinsmen came as occasion arose.

On the next morning a larger body of matrikin, again led by their clan priest, assembled in the ward square bringing palm wine, kola and a goat. Many men and some women of the patriclan joined them amid a crowd of onlookers. The matriclan priest spoke formally, saying that Oka, the dead patriclan head, had been given by them to the patriclan for which he had done many good things, that the patriclan and all the village should deal fairly with people of his matriclan and that there should be peace. The goat was handed over to be killed by a patriclansman who was an okpan (a son of a matriclansman—in this case the son of the dead man), and the more senior among both sets of kinsfolk went to the compound where one portion was given to the patriclan and the two groups feasted separately in the compound.

The matrikin elders then announced the man who would act as the Burier for the matrikin. They had not chosen, as was customary, one of the more senior men of their lineage, but one of the younger sons of Oka's own sister. It was known that they had feared that unless one of them were given formal responsibility, these sister's sons might appropriate Oka's yam harvest and cause other trouble. At the same time, a vigorous man was needed to resist excessive demands that might be made by outsiders.

The matrikin Burier then declared to the patrikin that he would deal fairly with Oka's wealth and called on the patrikin not to conceal any of it. The patriclan elders, for their part, had followed custom in choosing as the Burier one of the older men of Oka's lineage but not any of his sons. He agreed to work peaceably and openly with the matrikin. A padlocked box of valuables which Oka had before his death entrusted to his sister, the mother of the matrikin Burier, was handed over to the latter. Some of the kinsmen of both sides remained with them both in the compound for the rest of the day to receive the other groups and many individuals that came. From these, as on later days, they received small gifts of palm wine and coins and to them they gave small portions of meat and kola.

Before nightfall on this third day, when the first visits of farewell and condolence were over, the body was placed in the grave without ceremony apart from inclusion of the conventional grave goods for a man.

The Rights of the Age-set

Some members of Oka's age-set in the ward had come the day before to be shown where they could stay. They were few, as he had been old and many of his age-set had already died, so that the duty of providing them with food that the widows cooked during the funeral period would not be onerous as it could be with a younger set. They were given the use of the third widow's house. Most came daily for food and a few slept there. Later, towards the end of the obsequies, they demanded their customary gift of meat and money from the widows. These should be given by the widows' sons who could seek help from other patrikin.

These gifts and services by the widows are thought of as repaying those which a man's age-set had rendered to them and their families at their marriages and also as concluding the obligation of wives to provide food for a man's age-mates when they visit him. On this occasion after complaints to the patrikin Burier that the widows had not cooked for them for several days and the payments had not been made, the patriclan Burier brought the widows to task and elicited the money gifts of a few shillings from each of them.

Succession in Ikpungkara

Oka had been the third in rank of the four heads (Oboi Yapkan) of the Ikpungkara association, politically the most influential in the village. Its leaders, with a few other members, had come on the day after his death to condole but also to declare their own loss and to announce that they would return a week later to be given their first feast supplies and to be shown the man who would succeed Oka as a member. This they duly did. All the members, some forty in all, assembled with their spirit bundles (akpa) in the ward square wearing their special waist cloths and fibre hats, and sent their messenger to the compound for the successor to be brought.

Oka had himself succeeded a patrikinsman in the association so that the right and duty to provide a successor and the admission payments lay with the patriclan although it could lay claim to some of Oka's resources for the payments as well as for the mortuary gifts to Ikpungkara. Had it been a case of matrilineal succession, of which there are fewer, such as those of members who are matriclan priests, the responsibility would have fallen entirely on the matriclan.

The Burier and the new Head of the patriclan[1] went out to meet Ikpungkara and, as was usual, put them off until the next day when they would present the successor and make the first payments. Meanwhile they gave some bush meat, palm-wine and kola nuts as an earnest.

Both the selection of the successor and the collection of the means for the gifts and payments had already been discussed in the lineage and among the clan elders. Oka's own lineage had first claim on the succession and the choice had fallen on one of his junior grandsons largely because he was known to have a large yam harvest of over 200 sticks and would have the means to contribute substantially himself to the admission payments. But he at first refused and accepted only after he had been given a promise of support from the patriclan as a whole and that it would collectively provide the first payment.

Out of the 400 rods which had to be found, most of those paid were contributed by other members of the patriclan and by the matrikin Burier out of Oka's money in the course of a considerable amount of dunning. Of the numerous goats and large supplies of bush meat, amounting to about the same value, which were demanded as gifts for feasts by Ikpungkara, some were provided by the patrikin Burier with the help of contributions from the patriclan. Some were bought with money belonging to the dead man with the matrikin Burier's consent and others were provided for the later feasts by the successor himself. Palm wine was contributed by men of the patriclan but the yams came from the

[1] The succession as patriclan priesthead of Oka's assistant (the Wine Pourer) in rituals at the clan shrine had, as was customary, been approved, meanwhile, by the elders.

dead man's yam harvest which had now passed to his matri-kin.[1] The son of the dead man, who had a strong interest in his father's reputation for wealth and generosity and was likely to have already received some money from his father before his death, provided most of the first payments with the help of a prosperous age-mate of another lineage who farmed with him. Later they recouped about half of this in many small contributions from other patriclans-men.

The Ikpungkara leaders had in the meantime been privately told whom it was proposed should join them and had agreed. The next day the new member came with the Patriclan Head and the Burier to the ward square, where Ikpungkara had assembled again. Wearing the costume left by Oka that was required for initiation—a woven raphia skirt, a striped waistcloth and a knitted fibre cap—he was placed on a stool while the two spirit bundles (akpa) were dis-played and the members circled round him silently in single file four times. The first payment, 120 rods and two live goats, was presented by the Burier and Ikpungkara marched off in file with the new member to their meeting house, where he joined in feasting on the two goats. All these pro-ceedings were carried out with great solemnity. During their processions and assembly in the square, as with all public appearances of Ikpungkara, other people had to keep out of their sight on pain of a fine which would be collected subsequently.

The new member was taken to stay with an Ikpungkara

[1] The current conventional estimate of the total value of gifts and pay-ments for a death and succession in Ikpungkara was £40. But little more than half of this was probably paid. On the other hand, this represented a large concentration and transfer of wealth at a time when the total value of household incomes averaged little more than £10 per year and barely a quarter of this was in the form of money. (See Forde (1946), pp. 44-64.)

custodian for a period and he joined in their subsequent visits to Oka's compound. They came ten times in all, first on the next day and later on one or more of the kokö days in each week, over a period of twenty-five days, to be given bush-meat and palm wine, while further goats and portions of the money were handed over. The goats for the earlier feasts were given in the name of the patriclan by its Head and the Burier, but the later ones were provided by the new mem-ber. During the night between its two last feasts, Ikpungkara made a long circuit through the whole village during which everyone else had to stay indoors and maintain silence, and its drums were played all night. Thus, through the cere-monies connected with the death of a member and the incorporation of his successor, its prestige and authority were asserted in relation not only to the kin-groups concerned, but also to the village at large.

The Ward Leaders and Kekpan of Ligwomi

Oka had been one of the nine members of the small inner group of the Yakamben in his ward which directed its activities and conducted the annual ward ritual after farm-clearing—Kekpan. He had had custody of the cult objects. The larger body of ward leaders, the Yakamben, headed by Ogbolia, came to salute him and dance in the compound before he was buried. On a kokö day two weeks later, the Kekpan group led by the Ogbolia came to the compound to remind the Buriers of Oka's membership. They asked for a goat from each of them with which to feast in honour of Oka, and an undertaking that a successor would be pre-sented by the patriclan for whose admission a cow, goats and bush meat would be provided. They were put off with a gift of bush meat and wine on this occasion and also again a week later on the grounds that payments to Ikpungkara had not been completed. When they returned a week later still, they threatened to bring their claims before the village priests' council unless the goats and the name of the successor were given. Finding a successor had involved selecting a suitable member of the patriclan, preferably one who was already an Okamben, and finding the money to buy the cow and goats. A grandson of Oka, who was young but respected and also had a large farm and agreed to contribute substantially to the payments, was proposed and accepted as an Okamben and member of Kekpan. Two goats were produced and handed over by the Buriers after palm wine had been drunk. Next day the goats were killed for a feast in the assembly house of the Ogbolia's patriclan and portions of the meat were sent back to the Buriers for Oka's kin in the compound. A week later the Yakamben came again to collect the cow that had been bought, largely at the expense of the new member, for £2. They sang the songs of the Kekpan ritual and invited the new member to join them the next day when the meat would be divided. He and his patrikin were authorized by Ogbolia, the ward head, to make a forced collection of palm wine for the feast from tappers returning to the ward that morning. Replacement in the cult group of the ward had been secured, and demonstrated in a feast at the assembly house of the ward head.

Gifts to the Head Hunters Association

Oka had also been a member of the association of head hunters in his ward which formerly ambushed its victims on the outskirts of neighbouring territories. Their activities had been much curtailed and were clandestine as a result of Government vigilance in the thirties, but it was said that earlier they had had the duty and the honour of providing human flesh for feasts and heads for placing in the graves of men of their ward who had been priests in major cults. Their organization and ceremonial dances continued. There was no evidence that they sought a victim for Oka's funeral, but as he had been one of their leaders they came after the burial saying that they should in commemoration perform their dances in the village and requesting a goat for their feast. The matrikin Burier consented. And some days later, led by the masked figures, one male and two female, and bearing bifid and broad-bladed swords, they performed in the square of each ward a dance that mimed the hunting down of a victim. At the entrance of Oka's compound the matrikin Burier had tied a he-goat which was then killed by the male masked figure, as if it were a human victim, during a further miming dance. Their feast was then prepared and held in the compound. For this the patrikin, who also shared in it, provided a large pot of palm wine.

Feasts and Displays for the Club of the Rich Men

The Epoli association of rich men in each ward took its name from one condition for membership, namely the purchase of one or more stranger children (yafoli). Such a purchase, which required payments to the value of several pounds, enhanced the standing not only of the purchaser and his household, but also of his patrikin and matrikin in both of which the child, usually a girl, would be incorporated as a daughter. The association itself had formerly promoted and safeguarded the foreign contacts needed for this traffic which had been considerable until the Administration had suppressed it in recent years. At the admission and death of a member the club assembled to display their wealth and be feasted.

Oka had been the head of Epoli in his ward and its members had come before he was buried bringing a token gift of condolence (epom) to his kin and to address him. Later they came to the compound to carry out their commemorative display for which his wealth in currency and cloth should be put at their disposal. For this the old currency of iron bars and brass rods should be used. The former were lashed together to build a cubical framework about five feet high draped in cloths and open on two sides within which the brass rods were piled up. There they were left on display throughout the obsequies until just before the final re-making of the grave that preceded the distribution of the dead man's property.[1] After erecting the display and being given bush meat and wine by the matrikin Burier, who was mainly concerned as the custodian of Oka's money, the members went in procession through the village ringing a bell and singing an Epoli song as they each trailed an iron rod. Contributions in money were given by each member of Epoli and also by the older kinsmen of the dead man, who were all visited. Returning to the compound, each member rang the bell in turn, once for each child he had bought, made a boastful speech about his wealth and the skill and energy with which he gained it, and ended by throwing his iron bar noisily to the ground. The matrikin Burier was handed the money collected as a contribution to the feast he had to give when Epoli came to dismantle their display at the re-making of the grave. For this, the husbands of the yafoli of the dead man had also to give goats and the Buriers had to provide, with the help of their kin, large quantities of palm wine to fill the large Epoli wine-pot which was brought to the compound. The husbands of the yafoli had also been told to bring smoked meat, palm wine, a kola nut and a pot of water for a ritual to precede the feast. In this the yafoli and their hus-

[1] With the replacement of the old currencies over more recent years by British West African coinage, men no longer kept most of their funds in bars and rods. But they were still valued and exchangeable for coins, and loans were also made to assemble supplies of them to perform in the customary way these and other ceremonies in which they should be used.

bands were joined by the leading members over the grave. While the meat was eaten, Oka, the dead man, was addressed and told that Epoli would see that his yafoli were treated well by his kinsmen. To secure peace and health for the yafoli and good will from all concerned, the water from the pot was then thrown on the front roof to trickle down on their backs as they came out.

Later, after Oka's grave had been remade and his goods distributed, both Buriers called their kin together to arrange for the Epoliti ceremony in which his wealth and his status as an Epoli member were celebrated and his death was publicly mourned. Money was collected from both sets of kin but the matrikin were expected to contribute most, and they did so, under some pressure from the patrikin. A cow and large quantities of palm wine were bought. The Epoliti was erected in the compound. This was a long bamboo pole on which a red-tasselled cap stuffed full of leaves was set beneath an umbrella. From it hung a long banner of cloth. The cow was killed and, while the men butchered it in preparation for the feast, Oka's matrikinswomen and the daughters of his matrikinsmen (yakpanen), who all displayed their mourning by freshly shaved heads and black stripes on their faces, took its freshly severed head in procession through the village. They were led by Oka's daughter ringing a bell and declaring that she had a rich father who had died. The cow's head and the long rolls of cloth carried horizontally on the shoulders of some of the women were signs of the wealth Oka had left to his kin and that they were honouring him.

Inheritance

It was nearly forty days after his death before the payments and feasts to the associations had been completed. Only then could the ceremony of re-making Oka's grave take place[1] and his goods be distributed. Early on the day agreed by the two Buriers, the elders of Oka's matrilineage, the matriclan priest, his sisters and sisters' sons, came in a party to the compound and 'entered the house'. All his stools, guns, matchets, cloths, ornaments and costumes were displayed on the floor of the house. The matrikin Burier proceeded to name those who should receive the various items among these personal effects concerning which he had already had many hints and demands. Of these goods a fair share was given to Oka's own children, his patrikin, even though, as usual, it was murmured that there were other articles that his sons had earlier and surreptitiously removed from the house. The amount of Oka's money was not declared. During his illness he had entrusted some of it to his sister, to whom he had confided details of his property. She had handed this and his locked box to her son when he became the matrikin Burier. He now said that he was keeping what remained as his inheritance according to custom, detailing also, as usual, the large sums he had expended in providing for the feasts of the patrikin and the associations and of the future needs of sisters and their children for which he would be responsible.

Later that day the matrikin went to the harvest stacks outside the village where the Burier distributed Oka's yams among them after telling of the large number that had had to be used for the feasts. Of the eighty sticks of yams that were still tied in the stack most were distributed to Oka's sister's daughter, her sons and daughters and the yafoli. A few were given to the priest of the matriclan and to his

[1] This involved packing down of the earth and smoothing the ground so that no indication of the burial remained and was done without ceremony by some of his patrikin while some older matrikinswomen sat by wailing. The Yakpanun staffs were then stamped on the grave site by two of the patrikin. This signified the conclusion of the obsequies and should precede any distribution of a dead man's goods to his heirs.

sister. But a quarter were sold to outsiders and the money was kept by the Burier as part of his inheritance.[1]

It will be seen from this outline of the main relations within and between the social groups concerned in the mortuary ceremonies of a man of considerable seniority and status in Umor that such ceremonial emphasis as there is on the loss by the kin-groups of one of their members occurs for the most part in connection with their external social relations. The Kekbun group within the patriclan conducts a ritual mourning over the grave but for this it expects to be rewarded by the matrikin. The two kin-groups hold small reciprocal feasts of condolence. But there are no rituals at their spirit shrines. The dead man is not ritually accorded any posthumous status in either group. For while he is thought likely to appear in dreams to chide and threaten if the ceremonies and obligations connected with his death are not carried out, there is no form of ancestral cult. But both kin-groups are very much concerned in meeting the demands and providing for successors in men's associations in the village or ward. It is the associations which use the death of one of their members to emphasize their importance and power through their memorial feasts which are provided for by his kin, and by the payments made

[1] The term 'stick of yams' refers to a vertical column of yams tied horizontally on raphia uprights to a height of about 10 feet. The number and size of yams in a stick can of course vary considerably but this is the Yakö unit for reckoning the size of harvests. It was thought that about 20 sticks had been used for food during the mortuary ceremonies. A harvest of 100 sticks is not large, but would be ample for a man's contribution to household and other needs. Harvest stores pass even more completely than personal effects to matrilineal heirs and his widows received no share of Oka's yams. They had their own yams which had been planted and harvested in the household farm. These they kept. As widows they had the alternative of remaining in the compound under the care of their grown-up sons and farming with them, or of returning to their own patrikin where they could join a brother's household.

to them for the admission of successors and the ceremonies they perform in this connection.

Conclusion

It remains now, in conclusion, to consider why the ceremonial activities and material demands of the village and ward associations play the dominant part that we have described in the funeral procedures of leading men among the Yakö. An obvious answer in general terms is that this follows from the fact that some of these associations have a leading role in the exercise of social control over the community as a whole and its main territorial divisions, and also because their members are men of prominence and means who seek to maintain their ascendancy in this way.

Such an assertion, however, raises further questions. How have the associations achieved this dominance? And why is this expressed in obligatory feast-giving and fee-paying succession from the kin-groups of their members at death? In accounting for the powers of the leading associations we have to note in the first place that the Yakö villages are large, often very large, compact settlements in which are closely juxtaposed a large number of separate and corporate patriclans with their several claims to dwelling areas and farm lands. The built-up area of Umor was already over half a square mile in the thirties. This has meant, on the one hand, that a considerable degree of co-ordination and co-operation between them has been needed to maintain orderly activity in the community and, on the other, that much competition and latent hostility have been engendered between them by the exigencies of that activity. Rivalries have developed with growing need for land and forest resources, and fears for the security of harvests and livestock have been real.

At the same time, however, there has been no single superordinate power or definite hierarchy of authority culminating in a chiefship to determine and control the rights and actions of patriclans and lineages in relation to one another, or, on the other hand, to compel their observance of the rules of matrilineal inheritance. The village head (Obot Lopon) is only a *primus inter pares* among the fertility priests of the matriclans. His office commands no powers or ritual sanctions that are not in large measure common to the other priests. But these priests as a group have a common interest, not only in the observance of the rituals for the fertility and prosperity of the dispersed members of their matriclans and thereby collectively for the community as a whole, but also in ensuring the recognition of the traditional rights of matrilineal inheritance. Thus they have not only developed a strong corporate sense, but have attached to themselves, and have secured collective control over, the priests of other village cults to form a sacerdotal corporation—the Yabot—with comprehensive juridical authority over the whole community. At the same time, as leaders of dispersed matriclans expressing an ideology of peaceful harmony, they themselves have lacked the means for the enforcement of their justice. For this they have come to rely on and recognize the coercive capacities of Ikpungkara, Okundom, and, in more specific spheres, other village associations, and also of the associations controlling periodic rituals within the wards—the Yakamben. The Yakamben have accordingly, in enhancing their secular authority, recruited not only the ritual heads of the component patriclans and other priests, but also men of standing from all lineages. The Yakamben in turn have recognized and used the powers of another ward association, Ebiabu, to enforce their judgments on recalcitrant individuals or groups.[1]

[1] See Forde (1961) for a fuller analysis of these governmental functions.

The compulsion exercised on the kin-groups by the associations, apart from the Village Priests' Council, to provide feasts and fees for succession at the death of a member, finds an explanation in the fact that the solidarity of the associations in pursuing their own and the public interest is constantly subject to divisive and disintegrative tendencies arising from the ties of their members to corporate patrilineages and matrilineages. For, unlike the kin-groups, their solidarity is not sustained by collective rights in a body of resources nor by inherited rights to wealth. The associations accordingly have a special need not only to ceremonialize their solidarity in feasts and distributions of fees among themselves, but also to assert this *vis-à-vis* the various kin-groups of their members.

Thus, to maintain the appropriate level of their membership of, and their prestige in relation to the particularist and potentially opposed interests of, the kin-groups, and also in view of the limited means of individuals to meet the material demands for feasts and admission payments on which their prestige in considerable measure depends, the associations have insisted on the provision of feasts and the presentation of a successor by the kin of deceased members, and on the responsibility of the lineage and clan concerned for providing these. They themselves or other associations linked to them have at the same time enjoyed the means of enforcing these demands. Since they have judicial authority and means of enforcement in other fields, they have been able to extend these for the maintenance of their own continuity and prestige.

That individuals and particular lineages often covet membership in the associations and may compete for the enhanced status and influence it may afford, has of course to be recognized at the same time. But the very fact of competition within kin-groups for admission and its high cost in the disbursement of resources might encourage rejection of the status, and compromise the authority of an association if it had not secured the recognition and enforcement of memorial feasts for, and of obligations of succession to, its membership.

THREE SYMBOLS OF *PASSAGE* IN NDEMBU CIRCUMCISION RITUAL

An Interpretation

by VICTOR W. TURNER

Introduction

CIRCUMCISION rites, called *Mukanda*, have been described for several West Central Bantu peoples, including the Lunda, Luvale, Luchazi, Chokwe, Lwimbe and Mbunda. The most complete recent descriptive account is C. M. N. White's chapter on Luvale circumcision in his *Elements in Luvale Beliefs and Rituals*.[1] Through such narratives we now possess a sound knowledge of the *Mukanda* usages of these peoples. These are typical *rites de passage* as characterized by Van Gennep: the boys are removed from their homes in the villages, circumcised, secluded for a period during which they are subject to special rules and interdictions, and returned to their villages as men. The Ndembu *Mukanda* rites exhibit certain special features, notably in the role and small numbers of the maskers (*makishi*) who first appear at a special rite during seclusion, and not, as among the other tribes listed, at the beginning of *Mukanda*. I shall give an account of the total ceremony in a book now in preparation. In this essay I want to focus attention on one aspect (the symbolism) of a single episode (the operation and rites of circumcision) of the *Mukanda* as it is performed today among the Ndembu people of Mwinilunga District in Northern Rhodesia.

In a previous article[2] I discussed the semantic structure and

[1] White (1961).

[2] Turner (1961*a*). Given originally as a Paper at the Third International African Seminar at Salisbury, Southern Rhodesia, in Dec., 1960.

properties of some of the principal symbols found in Ndembu ritual and distinguished between three 'levels' or 'fields' of meaning possessed by such symbols. I pointed out that many ritual symbols are *multivocal* or *polysemous*, i.e. they stand for many things at once. Each has a 'fan' or 'spectrum' of referents, which tend to be interlinked by what is usually a simple mode of association, its very simplicity enabling it to interconnect a wide variety of *significata*. In this article I propose to consider three such polysemous ritual symbols (which form a series in a typical *rite de passage*), firstly on the level of their *exegetical meaning*, secondly of their *operational meaning*, and thirdly of their *positional meaning*. The first level, briefly, represents the interpretations of indigenous informants, the second results from equating a symbol's meaning with its *use*, by noting what Ndembu do with it, and not only what they say about it, while the third level of meaning is found in examining a symbol's relationship to others belonging to the same complex or *gestalt*. Finally I hope to demonstrate the usefulness of this set of methodological tools in exposing the deeper layers of a society's system of values.

The Circumcision Rites

The set of three symbols to be examined in these terms may well be described as the symbolic nucleus of the Ndembu boys' circumcision rites. For these symbols play a dominant role at the time of and immediately after the operation of circumcision itself. The symbols are trees of different species, *mudyi* (Diplorrhyncus mossambicensis), *muyombu* (Kirkia acuminata), and *mukula* (Pterocarpus angolensis).[1] Each may be said to represent a stage or 'station' in the novice's passage

---

[1] It will be shown to be symbolically important that *mudyi* secretes a milky white latex, that *muyombu* has white wood, and that *mukula* exudes a dusky red gum.

from social infancy to social maturity. At each of these 'stations' a series of actions are performed by persons enacting ritual roles. Furthermore, each tree is associated with a cluster of symbolic objects. Finally, the passage from *mudyi* to *mukula* over *muyombu* is regarded as a unitary process, with a simple meaning. This meaning stands in contrast to the multiplicity of senses possessed by the items and clusters of items at each tree station. What happens is that novices are circumcised under a selected *mudyi* tree growing in the bush, carried over a transplanted *muyombu* tree and made to sit in a row upon a freshly cut *mukula* log until their wounds cease to bleed. In the course of this simple process of transition from tree over tree to tree, each novice is regarded as having grown up (*Ku-kula*, from which *mukula* is derived, signifies 'to grow up'). The implications of 'growing up' are multitudinous, and it is here that one has to consider the senses possessed by the symbolic items.

I have observed only a single performance of *Mukanda*, for these rites are rarely performed nowadays, but I observed it in close detail, and I have many vernacular texts on different aspects of the rites and their symbolism. My procedure in this article will be first to present some texts relating to circumcision and its accompanying rites, to comment on them briefly, and then to examine the native exegesis of the three main tree symbols. I shall consider interpretations of these symbols both in the context of *Mukanda* and in other ritual and therapeutic contexts where they occur. Next I shall examine the symbols on the operational level, using both texts and observations as primary data. Finally, the positional meaning of each symbol will be inferred from its relationship with other symbols in the circumcision site. When this exploratory and expository task is completed I shall suggest how the interconnected symbols might be interpreted by the anthropologist.

Before the texts are cited it is necessary to say a little about the events immediately preceding circumcision. This operation takes place on the second day of *Mukanda* proper. The previous day has been a day of mobilization. Novices, their parents, kin and fellow-villagers have assembled from all the villages of a vicinage (a cluster of neighbouring villages); the circumcisers have arrived; during the night 'everyone must stay awake dancing and singing the *ng'ung'u* song of circumcision'. Just after their arrival the circumcisers poured out before the assembly the grey powder of their lodge medicine called '*nfunda*' after the baskets in which it is kept. *Nfunda* is believed to protect the boys from danger, disease and witchcraft during the three months or more of seclusion which follow circumcision.

The Events of Circumcision Morning as Ndembu see them

My first text (called A) describes the events of the morning of circumcision:

A

1. '*Chikukucha itang'wa tu-u, anyadi hiyakudya nshima de-e.*
   'Just at sunrise, the novices eat up the cassava mush completely.
2. *Hikubusa nukubusa Mukanda ni jing'oma ni jifunda ni lwalu*
   [Officials] select a site for *Mukanda* with drums, with *nfunda* containers and a flat round winnowing basket.
3. *Hikubusa hikuya kushikena, nfunda jejima chipu jiyedi*
   They select the site and prepare for the arrival [of the novices], they put all the *nfunda* baskets, two
4. *chipu yimu chipu jisatu chipu jiwana hikwinka mulwalu.*
   or one or three or four in a flat round winnowing basket.
5. *Kuteta iyala na mumbanda, hikukobeka kulwalu kunsewu kulwalu.*

They cut [in wood] a man and a woman [in effigy], and fasten them in the winnowing basket at the arrow.

6. *Hikukoka manfuntanyima hikukoka ni nfunda ni lwalu. An-shali*

They drag the *nfunda* basket and the winnowing basket backwards. The remaining

7. *ambimbi enda atala kwatela kukokela ni Mukanda.*

circumcisers go to look for a place where they should be dragged for *Mukanda*.

8. *Kushika nawu henahanu dihu hatela kushikena, henahanu hef-wilu*

They arrive and say, "This place is a suitable one in which [to await] the arrival [of the novices], this is the place of dying,

9. *himudyi. Neyi dihu Mukanda wekwawu mwatena wamu-yombu hikuya*

this is the *mudyi* tree." If the site of another *Mukanda* ritual is mentioned where there is a *muyombu* tree, they go

10. *na kuteta ni kushimika mwenamuna mwifwilu muna.*

and cut [it down] and plant it there in that [new] place of dying.

11. *Hikuya nakukeng' a kampobela nakukakela nakwinka mwif-wilu.*

They go to look for a *kampobela* fruit to clasp it firmly and put it in the place of dying.

12. *Kunona iyala na mumbanda akumani kwishina dakampobela kwishina*

They take the [effigies of] man and woman and put them under the *kampobela*, the man below

13. *iyala na mumbanda hewulu. Kunona nsewu hikushimika*

and the woman above. They take the arrow and insert it upright

14. *kweniku ku muyombu iku. Kuleta chikomu kikupapa kweniku*

here at this *muyombu* tree. They bring a *chikomu* peg and hammer it in here.

15. *Chikomu chimu ichi chikwawu ichi; chikomu diyu chikang'-anjamba*

One peg is of one kind of wood, the other of another; one is made of *chikang' anjamba*,

16. *chikoli ni kaleng'ang'ombi, ona wamung'enji waleteli Muk-anda,*

[that is,] of *chikoli* [wood], another of *kaleng'ang'ombi* [wood] that of the stranger who brought *Mukanda*,

17. *ni chikwata ona wakwatang'a, ni ileng'i dina datapana.*

and of *chikwata* wood, that which catches, and *ileng'i*, which pierces [or kills].

18. *Didu ifwilu dinamani tohu. Kaletenu nyana, Kambanji*

That place of dying is completely prepared. "Bring the children." [The novice called] the Warleader

19. *wakutachika kutapila mwifwilu ni Mwanta waMukanda ni Kaselantanda*

is the first to be "killed" in the place of dying, then the Chief of *Mukanda*, then the Rising Morning Star.

20. *Hikutetesha nyana yejima.'*

They get all the children cut [circumcised].'

A text [B] from another informant takes up the narrative. After describing how greatly speed is valued as a circumciser's talent, the text continues:

B

1. *'Neyi anyadi ejima anamani dehi akuyishakamisha kumutondu*

'When all the novices are finished, i.e. circumcised, [the senior men] make them sit down on a tree,

2. *wawulehi wututa wa mukula. Ayilombola aletang'a*

long and freshly cut, of *mukula* [wood]. The shepherds bring

3. *yitumbu yakusesa yamafulu amupuchi akwinka muchizanda*
   medicines made from the outer bark and the leaves of the
   mupuchi tree, put them in a potsherd
4. *nakuyikamwina kumawuyala awanyadi ejima. Neyi mashi*
   anamani
   and squeeze them on the penes of all the novices. When
   the blood has finished
5. *kuhita, ayilombweji akuleta yitumbu yikwawu yakulamba*
   flowing [lit. "passing"], the shepherds will bring a different medicine [of a] soothing [nature]
6. *nakukasaku njing'amuki nakachilondu kantesha.'*
   and tie a very small piece of *musamba* bark-cloth round
   [the penes].'

Commentary

Like many other native descriptions of ritual these texts are
highly compressed and elliptical. They describe in effect
how the site of circumcision—'the place of dying'—is prepared. Later, when we consider the operational and positional meaning of the three station-symbols, we shall find
that much detail has been omitted from these informants'
accounts. But the broad outlines are there, and the detail is
implicit. To put the rites of the three stations in their proper
perspective it will be necessary to consider some of these
implications. Consequently, I have numbered each line
of the two texts A and B in order to make interpretation
easier.

A. *The Exegetical Level of Meaning*

I have laid early stress on the relations between the three
station-symbols in order that these may not be obscured by
the detailed exegesis of each symbol. For each symbol, as I
have indicated earlier, is itself a system of referents which
cover many aspects of Ndembu life and culture.

1. *Mudyi*

The first symbol we shall consider at this level is the *mudyi* tree. I have written at some length elsewhere about the meaning of *mudyi*[1] in the context of the Ndembu girl's puberty rites (*Nkang'a*). There it signifies [1] maternal milk and breasts—from the milky latex secreted by the tree; [2] a mother and her child; [3] a matrilineage—that of the novice in the puberty rites; [4] matriliny—the principle of descent through women from a matrilineal ancestress; [5] the tribe or tribal custom (literally 'our kind', *muchidi wetu*); [6] 'women' as a category, contrasted with 'men'; [7] womanhood;

In discussing the procedure and symbolism of *Mukanda* with informants I obtained much the same kind and ranges of interpretations of *mudyi* as in *Nkang'a*. I shall discuss the operational meaning of *mudyi* in *Mukanda* as a 'place of suffering' or trial presently. But first I would like to assemble some indigenous interpretations of *mudyi* with reference to its use in other kinds of ritual, and in some therapeutic contexts.

The Mother–Infant Tie

Mudyi symbolism is closely associated with the bond between a mother and her small infant, and even with her unborn foetus. Thus, if a baby dies it is buried beneath a *mudyi* tree. A prematurely born foetus is also buried under a *mudyi* and *mudyi* leaves are put in the grave, which is a shallow one. Ndembu women say that if the foetus were buried in the usual 'red grave' (*kalung'a kachinana*) prepared for adults, the mother would never bear another child. In explanation of these *mudyi* burials it was said that 'only when a baby has drunk very much milk does it possess an ancestor spirit

---

[1] Turner, *op. cit., passim.*

(*mukishi*); if it dies when it is tiny, it has no *mukishi*. Therefore, it is buried in a *mudyi* grave.' But if the infant has no
mukishi, it is believed to possess *wumi*, which may be regarded as a generic life-principle. For example, in the
Kaneng'a ritual, performed to exorcize familiars of sorcery
and witchcraft, 'medicine (*yitumbu*) is collected', said one informant, 'from the *mudyi* trees where dead infants are laid.
This is because *mudyi* is where life (*wumi*) is, the life of dead
children.' Such medicine is collected to show any witches or
sorcerers present that they have been found out (literally,
'known'), since 'witches think of people's graves as places
where they get their meat quickly', for Ndembu witches are
necrophagous.

The placenta and umbilical cord are also buried under
mudyi sticks. As one woman informant told my wife: 'After
a birth the woman's husband collects ten or twelve sticks of
mudyi wood and gives them to the midwife who digs a small
hole behind the woman's hut. She then places the placenta
in the hole, and covers it with the *mudyi* sticks placed side by
side horizontally. Four sticks are planted upright at the cor-
ners to keep dogs out. The umbilical cord is also buried
under this with one end left sticking out of the ground. If
the whole cord is put underground, the woman will not
have another baby.'

A possibly analogous practice may be found in the custom
of burying a hunter in a sitting position with a *mudyi* pole
touching his brow and emerging from his grave. Blood is
poured down this pole by hunter kinsmen of the deceased
when they make a kill, and these offerings are believed to
'feed' him (*kumudyisha*). *Mudyi* symbolism plays a not incon-
siderable part in hunting ritual. For example, in a form of
invocation to ancestor spirits known as *ku-pandula*, a leaf of
mudyi is placed on the back of one hand and smartly
smacked with the palm of the other. Then the spirit is ex-

horted to help his hunter relative. Why is *mudyi* used? Here
is a hunter's answer: 'Because *mudyi* represents that part of a
woman from which everyone came, her breasts. It is explained by *Nkang'a*—the novice will bear children, some of
them must be hunters, *mudyi* therefore stands for women as
mothers. A novice goes to sleep at *mudyi* [this refers to the
custom of placing a novice at *Nkang'a* under a pliant young
mudyi sapling, wrapped in a blanket, and forcing her to
remain there motionless for a whole day, while women and
girls dance round the *mudyi*]. Thus the use of *mudyi* in hunting ritual (*Wubinda*) comes from women that bear hunters
and men of lust [*wuvumbi*].' The last reference is to a
hunters' praise-song in which the sexual prowess of hunters
is extolled—'We want [as a hunter] a man who can sleep
with ten women in one day.'

Further references to the mother–infant link in *mudyi* may
be found in various episodes of the *Nkang'a* ritual. For example, one of the two upright poles of the novice's seclusion
hut is made of *mudyi* wood,[1] so that 'the novice may bear
children well'. A miniature bow, draped with white beads
representing 'children', is placed inside the seclusion hut
where these poles are tied together at the top. This is of
mudyi wood and stands for the novice's hoped-for fertility
(*lusemu*). Here it might be worth noting that several ways of
representing female fertility meet in the *mudyi*-bow symbol.
A bow (*wuta*) is feminine, [a] because it is shaped like a con-
tainer—gourds and calabashes are regarded as womb-symbols
in divination,[2] and [b] because it is held in the left hand,
while the arrow is held in the right. The arrow (*nsewu*) is
masculine. The term for marriage-payment is *nsewu*, and in
the circumciser's medicine-basket two arrows are inserted at

[1] The other is of *mukula* wood.
[2] See my *Ndembu Divination: Its Symbolism and Techniques* (1961),
p. 11.

each end, representing *wuyala*, which means both 'masculinity' and 'penis'. Thus the miniature bow (*kawuta*) of *mudyi* wood is a highly condensed symbol for fruitful womanhood. More than this it re-establishes the connection, just noted, between hunting and female reproduction. I have no space in this article to exhibit the full range of correspondences which Ndembu make between hunting and giving birth—the same symbols are used for a multiplicity of kills and a multiplicity of children. Behind both activities is the idea of nourishment—many kills mean much food, much food means plenty of milk for many children.

The leaves of the novice's *mudyi* tree represent children in *Nkang'a*. Towards the end of the rites of *Kwing'ija*, 'causing to enter', the first day of the puberty ritual, women take a leaf apiece from the *mudyi* tree and race one another to thrust them into the thatch of the novice's mother's hut in the village. The women say that if this is not done the novice will have no children. They say further that they are 'joining the grandmother to the grandchildren', in other words, perpetuating the matrilineage.

I have frequently heard it said that if a mother dies in childbirth a supply of milk may be induced in the maternal grandmother by washing her nipples in a mixture of *mudyi* latex and water. The same mixture will stimulate the flow of milk in a mother of twins who has insufficient milk for both. In these beliefs we encounter once more the association between *mudyi*, milk, matrilineal continuity, the grandmother–grandchild link, and exuberant fertility [twins].

Sexual Attractiveness in Marriage

Mudyi is also used in *Nkang'a* to enhance the sexual attractiveness of the novice. The powdered outside bark of a *mudyi* is rubbed on her vulva by her instructresses during the seclusion period. This is said to 'blacken' it. Black is the colour, not only of death, but also of sexual lust and adultery, (which sometimes lead to murder and sorcery) in the idiom of Ndembu colour symbolism. But in *Nkang'a* libidinous feeling is, as it were, made to subserve the end of procreation within marriage; it is 'domesticated' into the service of society, to employ a telling term of Professor Fortes'. This is expressed in the employment of *mudyi*, and not of other known blackening agencies, as a cosmetic.

Medicinal Uses

Finally *mudyi* is used as a medicine to cure leprosy. Here the bark of a *mudyi* tree growing in an abandoned *Mukanda* 'place of dying' (*ifwilu*) is used. The whiteness of the latex is compared with the whiteness of the spots and stripes produced by leprosy. Leprosy is one of the sanctions against breaking many of the ritual interdictions of *Mukanda*. Here *mudyi* seems to be used as a homeopathic medicine, according to the principle that 'like cures like'. *Mudyi* leaves also figure as ingredients in medicines used to heal circumcision scars.

Finally, I must quote again a text I have cited elsewhere, since it bears closely on the role of *mudyi* in both boys' and girls' initiation rites: '*Mudyi* is the place of all mothers; it is the ancestress (*nkakulula*) of men and women. It is the place where our ancestress slept; to be initiated (*ku-tembwisha*) there means to become ritually pure or white (*ku-tooka*). An uninitiated girl, a menstruating woman or an uncircumcised boy is called "one who lacks whiteness or purity" (*wuna-bulakutooka*).'

We have in *mudyi* what is clearly a formidable semantic system. The clue that connects its several senses is the notion of milk and the white colour of milk. The most sensuous and the most abstract are united in a single representation. The pure undifferentiated life (*wumi*) of the suckling is equated with the life of the novice circumcised under the *mudyi* tree. The simplicity of the mother–babe relationship is identified with the complexity of matriliny, with its many rights and obligations. Primordial feeling and desire, involved in the infant's relationship with the mother, are superimposed on the sense of duty, inherent in membership of a corporate matrilineage and of corporate local groupings with matrilineal nuclei. And it is by no mere disease of the analogical propensity that an equivalence is made between the whiteness of milk, the whiteness of ritual purity, and the whiteness of leprosy. For it is well known that the sacred, the numinous, the holy, are dangerous as well as beneficent. To come into contact with them at times and places and in ways unspecified by priestly authority or ritual custom is to invite disaster. For not only is a sacred object, such as *mudyi*, a concentration of significance, but it is also a concentration of 'power'.[1] Each of the things, relations and activities it represents is associated with a degree of power outside ritual situations. When these different powers are mobilized and focused on a single object in ritual, the single resultant power is felt to be quite overwhelming. Thus, Ndembu say that a novice is wrapped in a blanket during *Nkang'a* partly because, were she to see her *mudyi*, she would immediately go mad. And in *Mukanda* boys are not allowed after circumcision to enter 'the place of dying' on pain of contracting leprosy or becoming insane. Indeed, only the older lodge officials are allowed to approach the *mudyi* tree there.

Shall we say, then, in all brevity, that during a *Mukanda* ceremony *mudyi* represents the quintessence of the nursing mother–suckling babe relationship, with its deep dependence of babe on mother? This would not be an entirely adequate interpretation, for *mudyi* has also been shown to represent

---

[1] Ndembu use the term *ng'ovu* both for physical and mystical 'power' and say that symbols 'have power' or 'are with power'.

matrilineal descent, which is a social, as well as a biological, bond of nurture and continuity. For each novice in *Mukanda* (just as in *Nkang'a*), *mudyi* is *his* matrilineage too, and stands for all those men and women to whom he is linked by ties of common descent. This group is his corporate 'mother', so to speak. He is to be severed from it, just as he is to be taken from his own mother. For a time he will belong to an exclusively male world, from which everything feminine, apart from a number of symbolic objects and activities, has been removed from view. He passes from a *corporate* group, based on the mother–child bond, into membership of a social *category*, an association of circumcised males (represented by *mukula*), and in his complete obedience to the seniors among them he becomes, paradoxically, an individual. For he has been liberated for a while from his dependence on the main jural tie of his society, the maternal tie. The like is experienced as a liberation from the common. The novice is made free of the male commonwealth of the tribe. Nevertheless, we shall see that this passage from *mudyi* to *mukula* has several additional senses, and one of these represents a transition *within* the bounds of matriliny.

This transition from dependent child to free and responsible male will be better understood when we have considered more closely the next station-symbol, the *muyombu* tree.

2. *Muyombu*

I was told by my informants at the performance of *Mukanda* which I observed that *muyombu* was used 'because the novices had died'. They also said: '*muyombu* is the tree we plant for our ancestor spirits (*akishi*).' Since they would say no more than this, i.e. that the *muyombu* was connected with the 'dying' of the novices, and that the novices were in some way associated with ancestor spirits, it will be as well to have a look at some other ritual contexts in which *muyombu* is used. I have mentioned that *muyombu* is planted in most Ndembu villages as a shrine to the village ancestors. Such ancestors are among the Ndembu almost invariably matrilineal kin of the village headman, through whom they are most typically approached.

Since *muyombu* among the Ndembu is even more closely associated than *mudyi* with white symbolism, I must first point out that Mr. White,[1] after describing the tree among the Balovale tribes as 'the protector of the village, and the seat of the ancestors of the living kindred', goes on to say: 'When the bark is cut, a dusky reddish latex exudes which symbolizes blood and, from other uses of trees which exhibit red latex of this type, it seems clear that blood is closely associated with fertility through the idea of menstrual blood, and blood in general as symbolic of life.' Mr. White does not state whether he is referring to Lunda, Luvale, Chokwe or Luchazi usages. The same Bantu radical may be applied, even by peoples living adjacently, to botanically distinct species. For example, in the *Check List* issued by the Northern Rhodesia Forestry Office in June 1950, the term *muyombo* in Luchazi stands for two distinct botanical species, *Markhamia lanata* and *Ricinodendron rautanenii*. In Luvale *muyombo* is *Kirkia acuminata*, while *muyombo wa bazhimo* is *Commiphora chlorocarpa*. Finally, in Luvale *muyombowazhimo* is given as *Dialiopsis africana*. The Ndembu [Lunda] term given in the *Check List* is *mwiombo*, meaning *Kirkia acuminata*, corresponding to one of the Luvale senses. The same radicals, *-ombo* or *-ombu*; *-ombwe* and *-yombu*, reappear in a number of other Northern Rhodesian tribal languages, where they designate a wide range of species. The term *mwiombo*, mentioned in the *Check List*, would appear to be the dialectal variant of the Southern Lunda term *muyombu* which is found in the Mwinilunga pedicle chiefdoms near Kalene Hill. If

[1] White (1948), p. 149.

this is the case the *muyombu* of the Ndembu is probably *Kirkia acuminata*.

This *muyombu* certainly possesses a dazzlingly white wood when its outer bark is peeled off. Ndembu themselves classify it among 'white things' (*yuma yitooka*), and interpret it as a white symbol. The tree secretes a colourless gum, which they liken to 'tears' (*madyilu*), saying that the person in whose memory a *muyombu* has been planted was once wept over at a funeral camp. And it is worth noting here that the mothers of novices at *Mukanda* bewail their sons as though they were dead, when the men snatch them off to circumcise them at the 'place of dying' with its *mudyi*, *muyombu* and *mukula* stations. The *muyombu* at *Mukanda* was planted, it will be recalled, 'because the novices died'.

I have been present on a number of occasions when new *nyiyombu* (the plural of *muyombu*) have been planted to village ancestor-spirits. When a new *muyombu* is planted, this act always forms part of the rite of name-inheritance (*ku-swanika ijina*). This rite is not one of positional succession for normally the social position of deceased is not inherited, but only the name. With the name, however, goes the feeling that the inheritor, no less than the *muyombu*, is a kind of shrine, a living memorial, for the ancestor. It is usual for a person to inherit a name only when he or she is considered likely to remain in residence in a village for a long time to come. The inheritor is known by the name of the deceased prefixed by the term *nswana*, 'inheritor of'. The name is thus kept alive and continuity is maintained with the village past. Thus one of the aspects of *muyombu's* operational meaning in *ku-swanika ijina* (name-inheritance) is social continuity. This aspect is clearly present in *Mukanda* too (see Text A.9-10) for the *muyombu* planted at the 'place of dying' is generally a cutting from a tree used for this purpose at a former *Mukanda*. Here the continuity is not so much a matter of names and social *personae* as of *rites de passage* giving entry into tribal manhood.

It is at the rite of name-inheritance that one finds *muyombu* most richly associated with other white symbols at the level of positional meaning. It is here too that native exegesis quite unequivocally attaches *muyombu* to the class of white symbolic objects. Among the other white symbols employed at name-inheritance are:

[1] maize-beer (*walwa wakabaka*)[1] or kaffir-corn beer (*walwa wamasa*). These are used 'on account of their whiteness'. They are also called 'women's beer', 'because of their mildness' (*ku-fomoka*) in contrast to honey beer (*walwa waka-solu*), which is considered 'fierce' (*wazuwa*), and 'a man's drink'. In name-inheritance, maize-beer and kaffir-corn beer are also called 'the beer of the ancestor spirits' (*walwa wawakishi*). Such beer is poured into a small hole in the earth made just in front of the newly planted *muyombu*. This hole is called *chinkudimba*. Holes in the ground have the general sense in Ndembu ritual, where they are frequently employed, either of 'graves' or 'fertility'. I shall discuss this womb-tomb identification in a later publication. Here it is enough to state that the ancestor-spirits, who inhabit graves or symbolic graves such as the *chinkudimba*, are also thought to have the power to bestow or withhold fertility;

[2] White smoke from a tobacco pipe (*mutompa*) blown by elders of both sexes over the *muyombu*;

[3] White clothing for the name-inheritors. This includes a white head-cloth, and for women white bangles; and

[4] Most important of all, lumps of white clay (*mpemba* or *mpeza*). *Mpemba* is the purest expression of the principle of

---

[1] Mentioned by White (1948), p. 150, as constituting the libation poured out when a *muyombu* stake is set up by the village head after a new village is built. White writes that maize beer is used 'because it signifies food'.

whiteness (*wutooka*). I say 'principle' advisedly for the Ndembu, essentialists rather than nominalists, believe that Universals, such as whiteness, redness, blackness, really exist and have power; they are not merely names. The three colour-principles I have mentioned are regarded as fundamental sources of phenomena and relationships. They are potent ideas which are expressed in a multitude of visible images and may be represented in ritual by many symbols. To represent them in ritual is at the same time to embody their specific efficacy. A white symbol contains the 'power' (*ng'ovu*) of whiteness. White clay (*mpemba*) is the closest Ndembu can get to expressing the essence of whiteness, whiteness *sui generis*. Many informants used the terms *mpemba* and *wutooka* almost interchangeably. I cite the following text for its typicality and because it gives just about the full 'fan' of exegetic meaning for whiteness:

'*Mpemba* is goodness (*ku-waha*). It is strength or firmness (*ku-koleka*). It is whiteness or good luck (*ku-tooka*). It is to have power (*diku kwikala na ng'ovu*). It is to be free from death (*diku kubula kufwa*). It is to be free from tears (*diku kubula madyilu*) [i.e. on account of the death of one's kin]. It is to escape being laughed at [mockery is the principal diffuse sanction against breach of kinship norms or taboos]. It is political authority (*wanta*). It is meeting together with the ancestor spirits (*kudibomba ni akishi*) [i.e. when invocations are made at the *muyombu*]. It is life (*wumi*). It is strength or health (*ku-handa*). Being white (*ku-tooka*) is procreative capacity (*lusemu*), it is huntsmanship (*wubinda*), it is giving [i.e. the habit of generosity]. It is remembering (*kwanuka*) [i.e. one's deceased kin]. It is to laugh (*kuseha*) [i.e. sociably with one's kin and friends]. It is to eat (*ku-dya*), for even if an unlucky person cultivates he will not have food. Whiteness is to multiply in children (*ku-seng'uka*). It is to make visible (*ku-solola*) [for secret, hidden things are bad (*yitama*), in Ndembu thought, and smack of witchcraft and sorcery].[1] Whiteness is maturity or old age (*ku-kula*). An old man has white hair—he is firm and white. If a person is caught by an ancestor spirit [i.e. afflicted with infertility, misfortune at hunting or illness by such a spirit], he is not unlucky, but lucky or white. For when the spirit is pleased [by having a ritual performed to commemorate it], it will give him good luck. Thus a spirit will punish a hunter for not remembering him, but after the hunter has performed *Mukala* [a ritual in the hunting cult] the ancestor spirit will help him to kill many animals. The *muyombu* is the tree that is whitened for the dead (*muyombu diwu mutondu wakutookela kudi afwi*). So also are the forked *chishing'a* pole, planted for hunter ancestor-spirits, and the small *katala* spirit-hut placed on termite-hills for hunter-spirits in the manifestations of *Mundeli* and *Kaluwi* [these are kinds of ritual in the hunting cult—*Kaluwi* is another name for *Mukala*]. Sweeping away dirt (*ku-komba*) is whiteness (*ku-tooka*). Washing oneself (*ku-wela*) is also whiteness.'

The concept 'whiteness' can be seen from this text to be a complex one, for it includes qualities [goodness, strength], virtues [generosity, remembrance of one's ancestors], the rewards of virtue [freedom from tears and mockery, fertility, living to a ripe old age], relationships [between ancestors and living, political superiors and inferiors] and states [life, old age]. Each of these referents is itself an abridgment of a whole system of concepts. For example, *kuwaha*, 'goodness', stands for good looks and for pleasurable feelings, as well as for moral rectitude. 'Whiteness' also represents ritual procedures aimed at purifying persons or places, such as 'sweeping' and 'washing oneself'. Here the process of 'making white' (*ku-tookisha*) is included in the notion of whiteness.

[1] See Turner (1961*b*), pp. 3–4.

It will be noted that much of the text was taken up with relating whiteness to the ancestor spirits. Whenever ancestor spirits are invoked or petitioned among the Ndembu the symbolism of whiteness is very much to the fore. Ndembu make such invocations on a number of occasions: at the first fruits of any major crop, such as a finger millet or maize, when the first calabash of beer is brewed from the new grain, before making a long journey, when a relative returns after a long absence, if there has been illness on an epidemic scale, for success in hunting, in thanksgiving for some favour. Before all life-crisis rituals, such as *Mukanda* and *Nkang'a*, and before performances of rituals of affliction sponsored by a particular village, the headman will petition the ancestor spirits to protect his people from the sorcerers and witches who are said to be always present at large gatherings. On all these and on many other occasions, the procedure is invariable. Either the headman or an important elder, male or female, of his village, invokes (*ku-kombela*) the ancestors at their *muyombu* tree, by mentioning the circumstances under which he is petitioning them and the favours he wishes them to do. Next he sweeps the ground around the base of the tree free of dirt, then he takes a piece of white clay (*mpemba*) in his right hand, anoints the *muyombu* with it, and draws a white line, or more often three or four lines, on the ground from the base of the tree towards himself. He then anoints himself with *mpemba* on the temples just by the eyes, 'so that he may see things clearly', on the brow, 'so that he may understand well', in a line upwards from the navel, 'so that his liver [the seat of the will and feelings] may be white', and on the outer side of all the principal joints of his limbs, 'so that he may walk well'. After this he anoints similarly those on whose behalf he may be petitioning and finally gives pieces of *mpemba* to all the other attenders at the rite, whether these are kin of his or not. In his petition he always

143

repeats at intervals the phrase, 'This is your *mpemba*', mentioning next the name and relationship to him of the ancestor
addressed. Sometimes, but not invariably, a libation of
'white beer' is poured out at the base of the *muyombu* tree
before the petition is made.

We have established that the *muyombu* is characteristically
surrounded by white symbols and connected with concepts
of purification. What of the tree itself? The answer is that
Ndembu make every effort to exhibit its white properties.
When a new *muyombu* is set up, the pole is stripped of bark
for about a hand's breadth from the top. The white circum-
ference thus revealed is then pared evenly all round with a
knife. Some Ndembu say that this is 'to make the *muyombu*
sprout better', for the quickset sapling planted as a shrine
must at first have no branches on it as a matter of ritual pre-
scription. 'It is one', as Ndembu say. Others say that this
exposure of the inner wood is '*like Mukanda*'. It is tempting
to speculate that Ndembu see in this act an analogy with the
operation of circumcision, but since I did not think of
making further enquiries on this point during my field-
work, I cannot bring direct evidence to attest to or to rebut
the hypothesis. What is certain is that Ndembu regard circumcision as 'making visible' (*ku-mwekesa*) a boy's manhood, and as cleansing from him 'the dirt of childhood'.
These ritual consequences would at any rate bring the operation of circumcision, connected as it is with two important
white symbols, *mudyi* and *muyombu*, within the semantic
orbit of the white symbolism.

Outside *Mukanda*, then, *muyombu* appears most frequently
in a context of ancestor-veneration. The ancestors here represent the ideal purity of the moral order. Unlike *mudyi*, however, *muyombu* is not connected solely with the *matrilineal*
ancestors. For a man may plant a personal *muyombu* near his
hut to the deceased relative, often a patrilateral one, whose

name has been allotted by divination to his child. The child is regarded as being under the special tutelage of the spirit of this relative, and as reincarnating some of his physical and mental idiosyncrasies. This shows that the values and norms associated with *muyombu* have a wider, more diffuse application than those represented by *mudyi*. They refer to the whole of a person's life, and not only to that aspect of it governed by matriliny. Whiteness is all that is open, honest, generous, pure, responsible and pious. It stands also for social unity, and for concord between the dead and the living, between traditional precept and actual behaviour.

A word should be said here about the circumstances under which new *nyiyombu* are set up, for the total meaning of a symbol comprises all the operations with which it is connected. Not everyone has a *muyombu* planted to his memory as a matter of routine. Only those ancestors who afflict the living with illness or ill luck are accorded such shrines. Although informants, questioned outside the relevant social context, give as the motive for such affliction that the ancestor spirit is angry because it has been 'forgotten' by the living, detailed knowledge of a village and its faction struggles always reveals the importance of sociological factors. These are of two kinds. Firstly, there is the aspect I have mentioned above of personal incorporation in a village community. Ndembu have high personal mobility, and a single individual may pass through half a dozen or more villages in a lifetime, utilizing links both of kinship and affinity to establish rights to reside in them. But there comes a moment in such a person's life when he feels that he wishes to settle as permanently as may be in one village, nearly always where he has close matrilineal kin. Here the second set of factors comes into play. I refer to the struggle, overt or covert, between factions of village kin, often segments of a single matrilineage. The leaders of such factions are always anxious to recruit members to their local followings of matrikin. Thus the aspirations of wandering individuals and faction heads sometimes converge. What then often happens is that the would-be settler falls ill and dreams of a deceased relative, someone who has not yet been commemorated by a *muyombu*, and the faction-head either divines himself or goes to a diviner, who declares that the afflicting spirit is angry because the villagers have forgotten him and will only cease to bring illness when a new *muyombu* has been set up in his memory and his name has been inherited by the patient. The village headman and the faction leader, if these are different persons, then conduct the name-inheriting rites. The new *muyombu* is added to the line of such trees planted to the dead of the matrilineal segment to which the faction-leader and the name-inheritor belong. But the whole village attends the rites, as well as many people from neighbouring villages. For the essence of the rites is unification and the promotion of solidarity, and it is believed that every group and type of group whose members are present must benefit in terms of increased corporate loyalty.

I discuss this operational-sociological level of meaning in order to show that the corporate unity represented by *muyombu* results from the overcoming of cleavages. An individual is incorporated into a series of groups as a long-term member—matrilineal segment, village, vicinage, perhaps chiefdom. Faction-struggle must be temporarily abated in the interests of village solidarity. But the cleavages and tensions remain latent under the manifest 'white' uniformity. And it is this implicit context of struggle which gives *muyombu* both its pathos and its power. This is why its pale exudations are known as 'the tears of *muyombu*'.

The solidarity of males at *Mukanda*, effected by the circumcisers' knives under *mudyi*, also hides multiple cleavages. For the novices are recruited from many villages, some of which are rivals for the prestige of providing important office-holders in *Mukanda*. To produce the *category 'anyadi'*, 'novices', *corporate* groups, such as villages—each organized round a matrilineal core—have to be robbed of their male children and aggregated together in a new way. Perhaps this is one of the reasons why *muyombu* comes after *mudyi* in the circumcision sequence. *Mudyi* stands for particularistic unity —the unity of matrilineages and villages, while *muyombu* represents a general unity—the unity of the moral order recognized by all Ndembu and sanctioned by the ancestor spirits.

3. *Mukula*

The third station, it will be recalled, at the 'place of dying' is a long log of *mukula* wood, or several logs placed end to end if there are many novices. Here the novices sit until the bleeding ceases.

Mukula leads us straight into the heart of Ndembu red symbolism. Informants at *Mukanda* told me that the red gum secreted by this *Pterocarpus* was called 'blood' (*mashi*), and that in this ritual it signified 'the blood of the novices' (*mashi awanyadi*). Later I discussed the symbolism of *mukula*, and its connections with red clay (*mukundu, ng'ula*), with two of my ablest informants. Just as *mpemba* stands for whiteness, so does *mukundu* stand for redness. The supreme biological expression of redness is blood, and thus *mukundu* also represents blood. And just as *mudyi* is an expression of whiteness and maternal milk in the vegetable realm, so also is *mukula* an expression of redness and blood in that realm.

Since *mukula* represents 'blood' in many kinds of Ndembu ritual, I must first discuss the Ndembu concept of blood [*mashi*]. Ndembu say that the blood of healthy people is 'clean and white'. Here 'white' is a term used metaphorically in the sense of 'pure', to describe blood that is untainted by disease. The blood that is attacked by disease (*nyisong'u*) is 'bad' or 'black'. The blood of a healthy person 'wanders about' (*akimbuka*) in his body. As one informant told me: 'to save a man's life, one must save him while his blood is wandering about in his body. If a body shows much pus (*mashina*), there is no chance of curing him, for pus means the decay of a person. Watery blood (*mashi amejimeji*) is bad (*atama*). An unlucky person (*muntu wahalwa*) has bad blood, people are not pleased with him. He does not kill animals when he hunts. He is sterile (*nshinta*). His blood is not seen [i.e. he will not produce children]. The semen (*matekela*) of such a person is not white or pure (*atooka*), but red (*achinana*). After the novices have been cut [i.e. circumcised] they are given sweet cassava mush. This is a symbol (*chinjikijilu*) of semen. There is no salt[1] in it for salt would give bitterness and pain to the novices. Well-stirred sweet-potato porridge (*ntamba jakufung'a*) is another symbol of semen. Sometimes white clay (*mpemba*) also represents semen.'[2] There are thus 'good' and 'bad' sorts of blood for the Ndembu, and indeed redness is a highly ambivalent concept. For redness itself can be tinged with either whiteness or blackness. Where redness has a 'white' quality, blood is 'good'. Thus semen, which is regarded as a form of blood, 'blood whitened by water',[3] is pure and potent. Where redness has a 'black' quality, blood is 'bad' and semen is 'red' or 'yellow', i.e. impure and incapable of producing children. Sorcerers and witches are thought to have these attributes. Others may possess them temporarily as the result of affliction by ancestor spirits or of the malignant attacks of envious witches and sorcerers. One of the aims of *Mukanda* is to purify the blood of the novices, since an uncircumcised person is known as *wunabulakutooka*,

[1] See pp. 159 and 165–7 for discussions of the meaning of salt.

[2] As at the *Wubwang'u* ritual performed to placate the spirit of a mother of twins, where *mpemba* regularly represents semen, and *mukundu* 'maternal blood' (*mashi amama*).

[3] The verb 'to urinate' is *ku-tekela*, while semen is *matekela*.

'one who lacks whiteness or purity', a term which is also applied to menstruating woman, whose periods (*mbayi*) are described as 'impure blood'. The term also refers to those who 'have dirt under their foreskins', i.e. to uncircumcised boys or tribes which do not circumcise. This dirt is called *wanza*, and to shout '*wanza weyi*', 'your dirt', at someone is to offer him a deadly insult. Thus to circumcise is to purify the blood and to remove that part of the male organ which is associated with infancy and uncleanness. It is also to 'make mature', and indeed we find that the very name *mukula*, the tree of redness or blood, is derived from *ku-kula*, 'to become mature or to grow older'.

When they refer to its significance in ritual, Ndembu say there are several 'kinds of blood', *nyichidyi yamashi*. (1) There is 'maternal blood' (*mashi amama*), symbolized in a number of rituals connected with women's reproductive disorders[1] by red clay (*mukundu*), *mukula* and a host of other 'red' symbols. In texts the phrase *mashi amama amawahi awunda* recurs, which means 'maternal blood is good and peaceful'. (2) Next there is *mashi awubinda*, 'the blood of huntsmanship', which is said to be 'inherited from both the father's and the mother's side'. This blood gives one the 'power to kill animals'. In numerous hunting rites it is symbolized by red clay and the *mukula* tree. The blood of huntsmanship is said to be 'good' (*amawahi*), and indeed in most hunting rituals white symbols play a prominent part, 'acting together' with red symbols, as outward signs of the invisible process of restoring to a hunter his 'power to kill animals' temporarily 'tied up' (*ku-kasila*) by a hunter ancestor spirit. (3) Then there is

[1] Such as *Nkula*, performed to rid a woman of menstrual disorders. *Nkula*, sometimes used as a synonym for menstruation, is also derived from *ku-kula*, 'to mature', and the *mukula* tree is the dominant symbol of the rites. Other women's rituals where red symbols are important are *Wubwang'u*, the Twin rites mentioned above, and *Isoma*, performed to cure women of abortive labours and miscarriage.

mashi awubanji, the 'blood of homicide'. It is to this category that the red symbolism of *Mukanda* is said to belong, *consensu omnium.* Thus the 'blood of the novices' 'goes into' the 'blood of homicide'. Other rites under this rubric include the *ku-tomboka* dance performed by a senior chief's hereditary war-leader, an official known as *Kambanji,* when he presents his chief with the heads of his enemies slain in battle; and the ritual, called *Wubanji,* performed to purify a man of the guilt of killing a fellow-tribesman or a lion or leopard, which might be the forms assumed by dead Ndembu hunters. The phrase often used to describe this kind of 'blood' is *mashi awubanji awulobu,* 'the blood of homicide is [a mark] of courage'. *Wulobu* is a difficult word to translate for it has the flavour of 'stopping at nothing', of immoderate boldness, even of admired transgression. The great champion of the Ndembu, Chipeng'i, who rallied them against the Chokwe and Luvale slave-raiders in the late nineteenth century was given the honorific title *Chilobu,* meaning not merely 'the Brave', but also 'a hell of a fellow'. Many of his deeds border on being misdeeds. In *Mukanda,* the red symbolism is linked, as might be expected, with the act of circumcision and its preliminaries and consequences. For it is the boys who are 'killed' and the circumcisers who are their slayers. One of the terms for circumciser is *mbanji* [allied to *wubanji* and *kambanji*], signifying 'a man-slayer'. The novices too are likened to war-leaders and slaughterers in a number of ways. The first novice to be 'killed in the place of dying', it will be recalled,[1] is given the title *Kambanji.* He is usually one of the older boys and is expected to give the others an example of valour (*wulobu*). One must not only kill, but also die, courageously. At the end of *Mukanda,* the morning after the boys have come out of seclusion, each of them, headed by *Kambanji,* dances *ku-tomboka, pas seul,*

[1] See p. 129, Text A.18–19.

before the local chief, headmen and lodge elders, as a sign that they are now real men.

I cannot refrain from mentioning here an interesting linkage between rituals associated with different 'kinds of blood'. Only persons who have shed the blood of men or of large animals are normally entitled to wear in the hair above the brow a large red wing feather of the Livingstone's lourie (*nduwa*). In ritual this feather is worn (*a*) by those undergoing purification in the *Wubanji* rites; (*b*) by adepts (themselves purified man-slayers) in these rites; (*c*) by adepts in hunters' cults; (*d*) by circumcisers (*ambimbi*); and (*e*) by novices at *Mukanda* when they dance *ku-tomboka*. In the last instance, it would seem that the novices are temporarily identified with those who 'killed' them; in other words they have been assimilated into the group of adult males on whose behalf the 'homicidal' circumcisers operated. In a sense, too, they may be regarded as having 'slain' their own childhood by their courage in having undergone the operation—for Ndembu maintain the fiction that the novices take the initiative in calling for the rites, though in practice it is their parents who inaugurate them.

A deeper level of identification emerges when we consider a further ritual context in which lourie feathers may be worn. This is during a ritual to rid women of menstrual trouble, *Nkula*. Here the patient wears a red lourie feather and is heavily daubed with red clay—as are circumcisers, man-slayers, hunters and novices. She is said to be possessed by and to represent the ancestress who, in the *Nkula* manifestation, caused her to bleed severely at menstruation. This spirit, too, is said 'to dance *ku-tomboka* on the patient's verandah' (in the words of an *Nkula* song). Here we find a cross-sexual identification which likens a particular type of barren woman to a blood-spilling man, and certain kinds of men, including novices in *Mukanda*, to menstruating women. Here the symbolism of *mukula* may appropriately be reintroduced into the discussion, for *mukula* does not merely stand for blood but the coagulant property of its gum makes it also for Ndembu a symbol for the scabbing over of a cut. In *Nkula*, it is said that a woman's menstrual blood (*kanyanda* or *mbayi*) should not flow away, but should coagulate (*ku-zemuka* or *ku-konda*) round the 'seed of life' (*kabubu kawumi*), implanted by the father, to form a baby. In *Mukanda*, it is desired that the boys' scars should heal rapidly. In both rituals *mukula* represents both blood and its healthy coagulation. The novices are implicitly treated like brides at their first menstruation.[1] The senior official during seclusion, the leader of the novices' shepherds—young circumcised men who attend to their needs during that period—and instructor in tribal mysteries (*mpang'u*), is entitled *nfumwa tubwiku* or 'husband of the novices'. He introduces himself to them by saying:

'*Ami nfumwenu, ami nasumbuli anyadi. Ami nukuyilama*
'I am your husband, I have married the novices. I will guard you
nakuyitala.'
and look after you.'

The term *mwadi* (pl. *anyadi*) is derived from *kwadika*, 'to initiate'. This term means 'to circumcise' in *Mukanda*. *Mwadi* also refers to the first wife a man marries, and thereafter to the senior wife of a polygynist. The cognate term *mwali* in other Central Bantu societies means 'a girl undergoing puberty rites'. Such puberty rites are almost invariably the direct preliminaries to marriage. Among the

[1] Among Ndembu the first menstruation usually occurs *after* marriage. The puberty rites (*Nkang'a*) are performed when the breasts (*mayeli*) show signs of development. This is connected with the proliferation of *white* symbols, notably *mudyi*, the 'milk-tree', in these rites.

Ndembu a chief is called *mwadi* on the night before his installation ceremony, and he is treated 'like a slave' by his people and reviled without being able to reply. In all these instances there is a marked element of passivity, of receptiveness, of 'femininity'. The chief is 'feminine' to his people, as an immediate prelude to assuming male authority over them. The novices are 'feminine' to the instructors and shepherds. Some anthropologists have mentioned homosexual practices between senior men and novices during seclusion,[1] among the West Central Bantu.

Mukula, like *mudyi*, is also a symbol for matriliny. I have many texts to support this interpretation, of which the following, recorded in connection with the use of *mukula* in the women's *Nkula* ritual, is an example:

'*Mukula diyi mutondu wakanyanda wakusema wamashi amama.*

'*Mukula* is the tree of menstrual blood, of parturition, of maternal blood.

Nsang'u yamashi amama; mulong'a etu nkakulula wasemini

[Here is] the story of maternal blood: on our account the founding ancestress gave birth to

nkaka, nkaka wasemini mama, mama niyena hakusema etu.

grandmother, grandmother bore mother, and mother gave us birth.

Diyu wading'i namashi alumbuluka. Indi chabulili

She is the one who has clear [or self-evident] blood. Without

nkakulula indi etu twadikumwekana kudihi?

the ancestress where would we be visible?

Diyu wading'i namashi alala achimwekeshu chejima,

She is the one who has true blood to all appearances,

Diyu iyenkeluwu kudi Nzambi kulonda etu tumwekani lelu.'

[1] See, e.g., White (1953), p. 49.

Those are the people who were given blood by God in order that we may be seen today.'

'Self-evident, true blood' is maternal blood, for Ndembu say that while a father cannot be certainly known, everyone knows who the mother is.[1] This is a kind of continuity one can rely on. Here again we have the value Ndembu set on making things visible, open, and true, on public knowledge rather than private secrecy.

Thus, although on one level the transition from *mudyi* to *mukula* represents a passage from social infancy to social maturity, from 'milk' to 'blood', on another level it represents a movement *within* the framework of matriliny. This movement may be likened to a shift from dependence (the tie of milk) on one particular mother or one particular *matrilineage* to the interdependence of adult men in a society dominantly articulated by the *principle* of matriliny (represented by the nexus of 'maternal blood').

To conclude this account of *mukula*—which considerations of space necessarily render rather sketchy—it should be pointed out that while *mudyi*, at the exegetical level of meaning, represents a harmonious and, on the whole, logically interconnected system of referents, *mukula*, at the same level, stands for much that is contradictory. This is a common feature of Ndembu red symbols, well expressed in the following text:

'*Yuma yachinana yakundama kuyedi, yela nikuwaha nikutama,*
'Red things meet together at two places, they act both [for] good and ill,
yadibomba, yikweti ng'ovu.'
they are mixed, they have power.'

Now it is a feature of relationships between adult members of a matrilineage among Ndembu that they are highly ambi-

[1] Cf. the Roman proverb: *mater semper certa, pater incertus.*

valent, for they have an aspect of competition—for office, prestige, personnel—as well as of co-operation. This aspect of competition and conflict may be ritually expressed in the fact that red symbols also stand for *mashi awuloji*, i.e. for 'the blood of witchcraft/sorcery'. This is the blood 'which is seen when witches eat human meat'. Since witches and sorcerers most frequently kill their *matrilineal* kin, according to Ndembu belief, there is probably more than coincidence in the employment of identical symbolism for 'maternal blood' and 'witches' food'. In the symbolism of witch beliefs, incidentally, Ndembu see a mixture of red and black 'things'; whereas in hunting cults red and white symbols are conjoined.

B. *The Operational Level of Meaning*

We must now turn our attention to what is done at the three stations and who do it. The *mudyi* is the site of circumcision, and with the operation four main social categories are concerned: circumcisers, novices, novices' fathers (*asanyadi*) and shepherds (*ayilombola*). At the *muyombu* shepherds and novices play the ritual roles. The *mukula* situation involves the first four categories again. The boys are circumcised at *mudyi*, lifted over *muyombu*, and rested, fed and treated with medicines at *mukula*. Women are physically excluded from the proceedings but participate in them by proxy in the symbolism of *mudyi*, *mukula*, and the female figurine, and from afar by gently wailing near the ritual fire in the bush between the village sponsoring *Mukanda* and the circumcision site. Their exclusion, as Professor Gluckman has shown[1] for the Wiko of Barotseland, is structurally meaningful in a positive way: 'The boys are ritually separated from their mothers to be identified with their fathers, and

[1] Gluckman, 'The Role of the Sexes in Wiko Circumcision Ceremonies', in Fortes (Ed.) (1949b).

their mothers have to assist in this separating process by surrendering their sons.' They are also separated from womanhood and incorporated in a purely masculine milieu for a time. Here it is worth while pointing out that in ritual the concept of purification often signifies purification of a single principle, element or activity of social life from everything with which it is customarily or pragmatically connected in secular circumstances. Among Ndembu it may broadly be said that each major kind of ritual gives plenary or ideal expression to one constituent, or a few closely linked constituents, of society, and excludes, or even expels, whatever is felt to possess a different essence. Thus the concept of pollution may have a situational character for the Ndembu. Contact between women and the *mudyi* tree is obligatory in the girls' puberty rites (*Nkang'a*); at circumcision, the homologous phase in *Mukanda*, such contact would be polluting and ritually dangerous. Yet, to repeat an important point, the exclusion of real women and mothers does not prevent the symbolic representation of the feminine. There is a tendency to dualism in Ndembu religion (subordinated to the tripartite colour symbolism of white, red and black) which though trans-sexual is frequently expressed in terms of masculine and feminine. This dualism 'breaks through', so to speak, in the entirely masculine world of the seclusion phase of *Mukanda*, in the guise of symbols and terms indicative of femininity and submissiveness.[1]

Throughout and just after circumcision the fathers of the novices act as their protectors. It is said that in the past a novice's father would stand just behind him, axe in hand, ready to deal the circumciser a fatal blow if he were to mutilate the boy. This primordial situation portrays the male world as divided into two camps. There are the circumcisers and their assistants (*yifukaminu*), who menace the boys and

[1] See p. 152.

who have threatened in song to devour them 'like a lion who eats by the path without waiting to drag his prey to his lair'. Ranged against them are the fathers and the shepherds. The latter may include the fathers of some novices, but are very largely recruited from the primary or classificatory older brothers (*ayaya*) of the novices. An older brother is recognized as a boy's father's deputy in many secular situations. The point here is that for the boys, the circumcised men are divided into two opposed groups, those who 'ill-treat' them and those who look after them. Although it is in fact the novices' fathers who have put them into *Mukanda*, these men nevertheless appear to their sons at this critical and shocking moment of their lives as protectors. The circumcisers bear the full brunt of the novices' aggressive and revengeful feelings. After the operation they are forbidden to approach the novices directly, but may speak to them from concealment only. They are hidden in the 'place of dying' which it is taboo for the novices to enter after the day of circumcision. The boys in the lodge, which is erected the day following circumcision, are allowed to revile the circumcisers as savagely as they like without reprisal or reply. That the circumcisers are restricted to the 'place of dying' when they wish to approach the novices—and this restriction applies even to circumcisers who have sons in the lodge—accords well with their ritual role as 'killers' and 'homicides'. The lodge is the place of recovery and growth, where the fathers and shepherds tend the boys and teach them the masculine mysteries.

At *mudyi* the circumcisers dominate, though their mastery is wielded with fear and trembling, for they fear the male kin of those they circumcise and know too that the speed and skill of their work is being compared with those of their colleagues. At the *muyombu* the shepherds, who bore the boys away from their real mothers and now bear them away from *mudyi*, the tree of mothers, come into their own, as the veritable agents of passage. And at the *mukula* the fathers feed their sons with cassava mush mixed with beans (*makundi*—a noun derived, say Ndembu, from *ku-kunda*, 'to love', and associated in several kinds of rituals with 'a love-feast', in which adepts eat a joint communion meal), and ply them with sweet unfermented beer—to 'cool' them, for strong beer, it is thought, would make the boys' wounds bleed unchecked. Although fathers and shepherds will, during seclusion, become responsible for maintaining the discipline of the lodge, they appear at circumcision as the loving guardians of the novices. Since the nucleus of Ndembu villages tends to be a group of kinsmen belonging to the very categories represented at the vital moment of *Mukanda*, i.e. full brothers and fathers and sons, it may, I think, be said that one of the 'functions' of the rites is to strengthen the sentiment of solidarity uniting these kinsmen. But mothers' brothers seldom send their nephews to *Mukanda* and even less frequently play the roles of shepherds and lodge instructors. Although the mother's brother–nephew tie is important for local organization, this tie is not given ritual stress in *Mukanda*, possibly because it refers to *matrilineal* continuity rather than to contemporary masculine cohesion.

The father occupies an intercalary position between several systems of social relations *vis-à-vis* his son. He is at once head of an elementary family, begetter of children for his wife's matrilineage, and representative of the authority-holding generation of males to the junior generation in a society where genealogical generation differences are structurally significant. The father bridges the transition from a boy's infantile dependence on the mother in the elementary family to a state which combines much greater independence from maternal control with acceptance of masculine authority in the wider social systems of village, vicinage and tribe. At the same time the father is not the one who snatches the son from the mother. It is as though the quintessence of masculine aggressiveness, embodied in the red-stained circumcisers, has itself seized the boys and 'killed' them, leaving fatherhood unpolluted by 'murder'. Indeed, throughout *Mukanda*, until the novices' scars have healed, a close ritual bond is believed to exist between the ritually segregated members of the elementary family. The parents of a novice are forbidden to have sexual relations. This extends to polygynous fathers and mothers with clandestine lovers. It is said that the flowing of the sexual fluids from the parents will make the boys' circumcision wounds flow anew. Novices' parents are not allowed to eat salt during this period, since salt tastes like blood, and, as we have seen, blood and seminal fluid are ritually connected.

This identification of members of the elementary family with one another in *Mukanda* betrays itself in several ways. In some contexts, as we have seen, the novices appear as the 'wives' of *Nfumwa tubwiku* or Lodge-instructor, who is usually 'the man who has sent most sons into *Mukanda*', and is, therefore, a representative of the group of fathers. When the fathers feed the novices on the *mukula* log, they enact a maternal role, for mothers feed infants by hand in just the same way. Just before the novices leave seclusion, the roles are reversed, for a lodge official, usually one of the senior shepherds, wrapped in a blanket, disguises himself as a woman called '*Nyakayowa*' and mimes copulation with each of the novices in turn. In the secret language of the lodge the term '*nyakayowa*' signifies 'woman'.

Mothers and novices are mystically connected during seclusion. At dawn and at sunset, either the novices in the lodge or their mothers at the sacred 'fire of *Mukanda*' (*ijiku daMukanda*) chant '*Kwalamo-o*' meaning 'Circumcision', and the other group replies '*Woho*', 'Assuredly'. The novices'

mothers cook for their sons during seclusion on the 'fire of
Mukanda', and after the day's work they sing:

'*Wujilang'a inyamwadi wujilang'a kudi anshindwa.*
'A novice's mother is taboo, *nshindwa* fruit [a euphemism
    for the female genitalia] is forbidden.
'*Hela kwila yuma yatama yamukunkulwayi mwaneyi hakut-
    wesa*
'If you do bad, worthless things [i.e. break the taboos]
    your son cannot
kwaluka swayuku hela wukukata musong'u mulong'a
heal up quickly or will sicken with a disease because
munamushimani mwana.'
you have behaved unnaturally [the same term is used for
    incest] towards the child.'

Thus there is no severance of the mother–son bond in
Mukanda; only a change in its character. Father and brother
are the 'figureheads' of a novice's 'transition' (to modify
Auden's famous line) from infancy to manhood. But the
family ties still hold throughout the change. The boys even-
tually go back to their mothers, but they return as men,
though often merely little 'men' of seven years old. Nevertheless, they are now privileged, as circumcised males, to sit
in the village men's shelter and hear cases being discussed and
to eat from the same bowl as the elders. They are no longer
'impure' (*wunabulakutooka*), but belong to the masculine
politico-religious sphere. They are 'sacred' as men, whereas
they were 'profane' as children.

When one compares the operational meaning of the
station-symbols with their exegetic meaning, one finds the
paradox that *mudyi*, interpreted as milk and motherhood, is
the scene of 'killing', while *mukula*, explained as blood and
killing, is the scene of paternal care and consideration.
Again, *muyombu*, the tree which usually forms the centre of

a petitioning group, has become a veritable mark of passage itself, over which the newly-'dead' novices are taken.

This contradiction between interpretation and operation may be explained not merely as a ritual 'inversion', but also as representing the transference to the father of the mother's protective role. Throughout *Mukanda* the weight of evidence suggests that its red symbols primarily refer to virility and male pursuits. *Mukula* represents, *inter alia*, masculine solidarity and unity. Here the boys' circumcision wounds are treated with medicines. *Mudyi*, the tree of maternal nourishment, dominates the scene of pain. It is as though all feminine attachments were being sharply severed from the boys and this separation were being vividly demonstrated to them. Indeed, both male and female informants have told me that the prepuce (*muvumbu*) is 'like the labia' of a woman. The boys are being 'made pure' by the removal of their feminine attributes—both physical and mental. This does not mean that femininity has an ascriptive impurity, but that it has a relative and temporary impurity, which must be eliminated if the boys are to develop properly into men. What is 'impure' for one category of persons and in one situation may represent what is 'pure' for another category and in another situation.

C. *The Positional Level of Meaning*

1. *Mudyi*

Each of the symbols we are considering is the most important constituent of a *set* of symbols. Thus, if we begin by considering the *mudyi* tree in its configurational context, we find that only a single small sapling is chosen (by the circumcisers) under which the first novice, called *Kambanji*, 'the Warleader', is circumcised. Some of its leaves are collected into a heap beneath it called 'the bed of *Kambanji*'. But other litters of *mudyi* leaves, as many as there are circumcisers operating, are placed at intervals of about a yard to the right of the tree. Such leaves are regarded as exceptionally strong '*mpelu*', i.e. items of contagious magic, and are sought after, so it is said, both by hunters and by sorcerers. For the blood of the novices falls on them, and 'adds to their power'. It may be supposed that the bloodied leaves represent 'killing' and 'death' and 'blood', and confer on their owners the power to kill animals and men.

A large round hard-skinned fruit called *kampobela* or *mukukampombu* (see Text A.11) is inserted in a hole in the ground just under the *mudyi* tree, cut exactly in half. Beneath the fruit are a couple of roughly carved wooden figurines representing a man and a woman, the woman being uppermost. On the flat surface of the cut fruit is placed a flat round winnowing basket (*lwalu*), and upon this is laid the *nfunda* baskets of all the circumcisers, containing the medicines which guarantee the safe discharge of their role and confer strength and virility on the novices. This medicine must never come into contact with the naked earth or it will lose all its efficacy. When these objects have been arranged the senior circumciser takes some 'white' maize beer, always employed, as we have seen, when ancestor spirits are petitioned, and pours a little of it into the *lwalu* basket. Then he puts in a leaf of the sacred *mudyi* for each of the circumcisers. These men, sitting around the *lwalu*, take their leaves and scoop up beer in them. They hold them suspended in the air while the senior circumciser invokes the spirit of the circumciser from whom he inherited his *nfunda* circumcision medicine. In nearly every case for which I have records this spirit was the circumciser's own father. Here we have another striking example of the importance of the patrifilial tie in *Mukanda*. A typical invocation runs: 'My father, you have taught me the things of *nfunda*. All my relatives are here. Give these circumcisers strength. Help the novices who will come. If anyone desires to kill the novices by sorcery, may it not be here today.' As the invocation is made the next most important circumciser holds the basket containing the *nfunda* aloft. When it is over the circumcisers pour the white beer over the small calabash containers of the grey powdered *nfunda* medicine. These containers, called *tudiwu*, are quite explicitly likened to the phallus. When this is done, they go to a meal mortar (*iyanda*) placed next to the *muyombu* tree and filled with pounded leaf-medicines to be applied to the boys' wounds. They take some of this medicine and splash themselves with it. Then they arrange themselves in pairs behind each litter of *mudyi* leaves to await the coming of the boys. Each pair comprises the actual operator and an assistant, called *chifukaminu* (from *ku-fukamina*, to kneel), who holds the novice steady from behind and keeps his legs apart.

All these actions and symbolic items have *significata* which affect the meaning of *mudyi*. I do not have adequate exegetic material on several of the symbols mentioned, but I have enough to show that the abstract significance of *mudyi* as a symbol of motherhood and mothering is qualified by the symbolic environment. In the first place, *mudyi* is treated as though it were an ancestral shrine-tree. This procedure is not unusual for rituals of affliction, each kind having its own 'dominant' tree-symbol or *ishikenu*. But the ancestors invoked are very frequently those of paternally linked circumcisers, not of matrilineal kin only, as the 'milk' symbolism might suggest. But here it must be remembered that *mudyi* is sometimes interpreted to mean 'our tribe' (*muchidi wetu*—see p. 131). Since the Ndembu regard circumcision as something which distinguishes them from most of the tribes to the east of them, it is clearly one index of tribal identity, though other tribes to the west and north also practise circumcision and claim to have 'come from Mwantiyanvwa', the Lunda emperor in the south-western Congo. Yet it is not directly to the *mudyi* that the circumciser prays but also to the *nfunda* medicine itself, that arch-symbol of virility. In *Mukanda* male things are lifted off the ground. For example, when the circumcisers dance in a certain fashion called *ng'ung'u* on the eve of circumcision waving their *nfunda* about and dancing in pairs miming copulation the novices must either be held aloft by their fathers or climb up trees—anywhere to be off the earth.[1] When the circumciser invokes his trainer's spirit the *nfunda* is held up and the ceremonial white beer—and whiteness can sometimes represent 'semen'—is also held up in the *mudyi* leaves. The *kampobela* fruit is spoken of by all Ndembu, even young boys, as 'standing for the sun (*mwana*)'. The sun represents all that is 'above' (*hewulu*). That is why the basket containing *nfunda* may be placed on a fruit which represents it.

We have here at the *mudyi*, then, symbols of both sexes, and of their union—the figurines of a man and a woman. I was never able to discover why 'the woman' was uppermost. No-one was willing to explain this except as '*mpang'u yaMukanda*', 'a mystery of *Mukanda*'. Perhaps we have in this an instance of that 'blocked exegesis' I have referred to elsewhere.[2] This occurs where there is sharp conflict between norms or between norms and wishes. We might see in this symbolism a representation of the enduring supremacy of matriliny over all male-to-male ties made on any other basis. Virility is a dominant value in *Mukanda*, but matriliny is the dominant jural principle. And although the father–son bond is stressed both in the invocation and in the post-circumcision treatment of the novices, nevertheless it is the mother–child bond which ultimately prevails in life.

[1] If they touch the earth, it is said that they will suffer from enuresis, i.e. regress to infancy.
[2] Turner (1961*b*), p. 1.

It is as though the union and interdependence of the sexes were being dramatically recalled just before the operation which will radically sever the masculine from the feminine. For the white beer, a 'woman's drink' as well as a sign for seminal fluid, is poured from a *mudyi* leaf, representing motherhood, on to the *tudiwu* phallus-shaped containers of the male medicine—one of its ingredients is the cindered foreskins of novices in former camps.

2. *Muyombu*

Masculinity dominates at the *muyombu* station, for as Text A.13–14 shows an arrow is inserted upright (representing the erect phallus) close to the tree. An arrow (*nsewu*) in many rituals represents masculinity or a man (see p. 133), and has no feminine connotations. Also at *muyombu* a peg, *chikomu*, is hammered in [Text A.14–17]. Several species of trees are used as pegs. One informant explained these features as follows: '*Chikomu* is a sign of strength (*wukolu*): it stands up very strongly. It may be the horn of an animal or a wooden peg. The thick-stemmed grass *kaleng'ang'ombi* comes from *ku-leng'a*, to cut into strips, and *ng'ombi*, a cow. The hide of a cow is cut into strips. It stands for the sharp grass which circumcised boys long ago. For there was once a woman and her son who went to collect some grass for burning into salt ashes. By accident a piece of sharp *kaleng'ang'ombi* cut round his penis. The boy fell down, crying. His mother, very sorry for him, took him to the men of his village, who said: "The boy must be taken away from his own mother and the other women." In that place they took a razor and cut the penis round properly, removing the foreskin completely. The father was responsible for his own child. Men were very pleased to see how the cut healed up, so they tried other boys. Just the same thing happened. The people began to understand that it was better for all men to be circumcised.

They danced and drank beer to celebrate the cutting of penes well and how beautiful (-*wahi*) they looked. That is how *Mukanda* began.'

Not only is *kaleng'ang'ombi* a masculine symbol but it also represents the mythological charter of *Mukanda* itself and gives an exegetical explanation of some of its features, such as the avoidance of salt and the separation of novices from their mothers. But other species from which the *chikomu* may be made are also not without semantic complexity. For example, *chikoli* [Text A.16] is of crucial importance in *Mukanda*. A *chikoli* tree makes the site of the camp where the kin of the novices sleep during seclusion. It is at this site that the 'fire of *Mukanda*' is kindled, where the mothers cook for their secluded sons and which will only be extinguished at the end of the rites. It is also the 'dominant symbol' (*ishikenu* or *mukulumpi*) for the rite of '*ku-kolisha*', performed by the circumcisers on the afternoon of the day before circumcision, in the course of which they prepare *ku-kolisha* medicine for the boys and their mothers. Both *ku-kolisha* and *chikoli* are derived from *ku-kola*, which means 'to be strong, firm or healthy'. The medicine (*yitumbu*), of which *chikoli* bark is the main ingredient, is employed 'to strengthen' people to face an ordeal. The circumcisers splash themselves with it, shortly before they wield the knife.

Chikoli is a straight tough thorn tree which blossoms exuberantly. One text I have collected interprets it as follows: '*Chikoli* is a very strong tree like the *mubang'a* tree on which the novices urinate when they stay in the lodge (*ng'ula*). Its wood is very hard. One of its names is *chikang'anjamba* from *ku-kang'anya*, to fail, and *njamba*, an elephant. An elephant fails to break it. Neither wind nor rain can break it, and termites cannot eat it. It stands upright like a strong (-*kola*) penis, or a man's strong body. That is why we say it means "strength".' *Chikoli* is used in *Kaluwi*, one of the rituals of the hunters' cult, as part of a medicine 'to strengthen hunts-manship'. Other informants corroborate the significance of *chikoli* as a symbol of virility.

About *chikwata* (Ziziphus abyssinica), another species from which ritual pegs are made, an informant said: '*Chikwata* is from *ku-kwata*, to catch. It has large thorns. A man's body stays well if he is caught by them. They catch him strongly so that the blood inside him stays strong.' In other words a man has to put forth his strength to escape from the thorns.

Finally, *ileng'i* is a species of sharp, strong reed, used in mat-making. Its ash, like that of *kaleng'ang'ombi*, may be used for salt, though it is reckoned bitter (*ku-tukuma*). In *Mukanda* it 'stabs' or 'kills' [Text A.17].

All of these qualificatory symbols are quite unambiguously masculine in character. 'Death into ancestorhood' becomes under their influence, 'death from femininity into masculinity'. It is appropriate that the plant which represents the mythological charter of *Mukanda* should be associated with a tree used typically for ancestor veneration. Later, the *makishi* masked figures which terrorize the novices when their wounds have healed are said to 'come out of the ground' near this *muyombu* tree. After affrighting the boys, they are led by officials to the *muyombu* tree planted to the ancestors of the village sponsoring *Mukanda* and are there given the names of remote ancestors belonging to the village matrilineage. The women are then told that the *makishi* are indeed those ancestors. The senior *makishi* give the novices' parents salt to eat as a sign that the boys' scars are healed. It also signifies that the parents may resume sexual relations, though their sons will be secluded for a further period. Here the connection between *muyombu*, salt, blood, ancestors, symbolic death, circumcision and sexual intercourse is clearly established.

3. *Mukula*

Finally, we must consider the positional meaning of the *mukula* tree. [See Text B.] After circumcision each boy sits on the log with his back to the *mudyi* tree where he was circumcised. A support of bark-cloth from the *musamba* tree is fastened round his waist to hold up his penis, and a small piece of *musamba* leaf is placed on its tip. This is done to prevent urination through fright. For the 'tying-up' (*ku-kasa*) properties of bark-cloth are believed to be communicated to the organ so as to limit the excessive flow of blood and urine. At some performances a long string of *musamba* cloth is passed over a line of small termitaries, one opposite each boy, and is set alight. The boys' members are held up in the smoke which, again, is believed to 'tie up' the flow of blood. The termitaries, frankly compared to penes, are scooped out on top, and the novices' blood is allowed to drip into the cavities. The bark-cloth symbolism modifies the *mukula* symbolism by emphasizing the coagulative properties of the tree's gum.

I have no space here to interpret the medicines applied to the boys' wounds. It is sufficient to state that one kind is to staunch the flow of blood and another to soothe (*ku-lamba*).

In discussing the operational meaning of *mukula* I drew attention to the role of the novices' fathers in giving them food and drink. Strictly speaking, the senior circumciser should inaugurate the feeding. He divides the cassava mush and beans into three small balls—explicitly compared to testicles—and puts them on the knife he has just used for circumcision, having first washed it in special medicine to purify it. He gives the knife to each of the novices in turn, beginning with *Kambanji*, the 'War-leader', and then to the other titled novices. Each boy takes the knife himself and swallows the food quickly. But it is customarily expected that the fathers grow impatient with the slowness of this performance and snatch pieces of mush from the circumciser to feed their own sons, regardless of ritual order. The significance of the feeding, besides indicating the 'love' that should exist between feeders and fed [see p. 158], is that each novice's strength and virility are being restored to him on the very knife that has just 'killed' him.

This rite of feeding the boys as they squat bleeding on the *mukula* bough brings out the significance of *mukula* as 'meat food', a sense it possesses in hunting rituals. It has this sense, too, in the seclusion phase of *Mukanda* itself, where a table (*kaweji*) of woven *mukula* twigs is placed to the right of the lodge entrance. Beneath it are thrown the remains of large balls of cassava mush sent by their mothers to feed the novices. These fragments are not disposed of until the end of *Mukanda*. If they are thrown away it is feared that the boys will lose their virility.

The positional meaning of the three station-symbols may be shortly summarized by stating that the boys are taken away from the sphere where both sexes interact, passed over the *muyombu*, representing the continuity through males of universal Ndembu values, and joined together in a community of male age-mates, who together bleed, heal and receive nourishment from the generation of their fathers.

The Total Situation

The whole site between the *mudyi* and the termitaries on the far side of the *mukula* log is known as *ifwilu* or *chifwilu*, 'the place of dying'. But this term applies more particularly to the *mudyi* leaf-litters where the operation takes place. Various terms are used for circumcision. One is *kwadika*, but this has the wider sense of 'to initiate'. *Kwalama* is a more precise term, but the verb *ku-ketula*, 'to cut', is very often employed. This term is also used in many kinds of ritual for 'to sacrifice' and refers to the beheading of a fowl. Indeed, in the *Isoma* ritual, when a fowl is being sacrificed in this way, the on-lookers sing the *ng'ung'u* song [see p. 127] of *Mukanda*, the refrain of which is '*kwalamo*', 'circumcision'. Clearly, the ideas of ritual beheading and circumcision are related in Ndembu thought. Thus, circumcision is a kind of beheading and a psycho-analyst might consider it a kind of castration, but, after all, it is only a symbolic and not a real killing, for elaborate precautions are taken to avoid the boys coming to any real harm and medicines are applied to heal them quickly. In other words we find in Ndembu practice some support for Père Lagrange's view[1] that circumcision is 'a sacrifice of a part to save the whole'. Only the foreskin is removed, not the whole member. Circumcision is a death to avoid a death, a castration to avoid a castration, so to speak.

The site of circumcision, like the scene of the girl's ordeal of lying motionless under the *mudyi* at *Nkanga'*, is otherwise known as *ihung'u* or *chihung'u*, 'the place of suffering'. This term is also applied to a hut where a woman is in labour. It is further applied to the hut of the senior candidate in an important ritual of affliction called *Chihamba*.[2] One infor-mant explained to me that '*ihung'u* or *yihung'u* stands for any kind of misfortune or illness given by a spirit because the patient has only completed the first, and less important, of the two rituals in each cult of affliction, *ku-lembeka* but not *ku-tumbuka*. *Ihung'u* can also mean any person who has been caught by an ancestor spirit.'

Thus behind the ordeal of the novices in boys' and girls' initiation rites is the implication that these sufferers have been 'caught' by the ancestor spirits, just as people are afflicted by them with illness or misfortune.

The 'place of dying' or 'place of suffering' has many

[1] Lagrange (1905).
[2] See Turner (1957), pp. 303–17. Also Turner (1962), section I.

aspects. It is the scene of symbolic death, or real suffering, of ancestral intervention, of symbolic birth and of prophylactic loss of part of the generative member to save the rest of it. It is also the site of a cluster of symbols which together represent a concentration of Ndembu values and norms. Since these values are portrayed in close juxtaposition to the operation of circumcision it would seem that the male member is being exposed to their beneficent influence. Thus one of the purposes of the rites must be to consecrate the organ of generation, 'making it white' and 'clean'. Ridding a person or part of a person of impurities is always regarded by Ndembu as a painful process, involving suffering of a reparative nature. Infancy is a 'dirty' condition, in Ndembu belief, and if men are not purified from it the intercourse they have with women will be polluting and unnatural (*kushimana*, a term also applied to incest and cannibalism), as I have heard many Ndembu say. Part of the filth of infancy is the close physical bond between an infant and its mother, a bond which seems to be associated with the possession of a foreskin and 'the dirt beneath the foreskin'. Women themselves are said to desire the breaking of this bond, so that their sons may 'mature' (*akuli*).

Circumcision as a Primitive Sacrament

A sacrament has been defined, within the Western religious tradition, as 'a thing perceptible to the senses which possesses the power both of effecting and signifying sanctity and righteousness (*iustitia*)'. It would not be stretching this definition too far to include within it most of what is meant by and goes on at *mudyi*, *muyombu* and *mukula*. For Ndembu do not regard these trees, and the other symbols, as merely speculative or theoretical signs, but as efficacious and practical signs, as instrumentalities, as they not only indicate the inner changes of moral and social status, but also effect them.

Furthermore, like the Christian sacraments, they point to the past, present and future, for they commemorate the first *Mukanda*, signify the various kinds of power they confer, and indicate the state of consummate manhood to come. Each boy is sacramentally imbued with the whole Ndembu moral order, which is immanent in but also transcends the social order, when he is circumcised under the tree of mothers, passed over the tree of ancestors and lodged on the tree of maturity. There are religious depths here that cannot be fathomed by the analysis of observational data. The symbols I have discussed have a fathomless lucidity of meaning which men of every grade of cultural complexity can grasp intuitively if they wish.

Conclusion

In this paper I have examined three linked symbols which deserve the term 'stations', for they constitute vital stages in a process, in this case the process of circumcision and its immediate aftermath. The examination has been made at three interpretative levels which, though separable, are interconnected. In considering the first of these, the level of indigenous exegesis, we are in the realm of native metaphysics. Each of the stations is treated separately and each of them represents a complex of ideas, ideals and sentiments. The second level is in effect a construct of the investigator made from his observations of ritual behaviour and from his knowledge of tribal social structure. The investigator analyses the composition of the ritual assembly and takes careful note of the persons and groups enacting ritual roles. His knowledge of tribal principles of social structure and his analyses of numerical data bearing on social organization are then enlisted. With their aid he discovers the links between the social aspects of the rites and the tribal social structure. At this level of meaning he must consider the symbols together in terms of the process which moves through all of them. The third 'positional' level of meaning (which is really an extension of the scope of exegesis from the single symbol to the configuration) considers whole clusters of symbols, centred on the 'stations', as ways of relating the aims and values of the specific set of rites to the total system of beliefs and practices. For each symbol in such a configuration brings into it a penumbra of associations derived from its use in other kinds of ritual, and even, in some cases, in pragmatic activities. At this level of interpretation a three-fold analysis is again necessary, but this time each station is not considered in its own right but as the anchoring element in a complex, each of whose items has to be interpreted and related to the whole.

If we combine these levels of meaning we find [as a disc, divided into differently coloured sectors, when spun turns white] that the semantic complexities of each level combine into a simple sacramental process. This process has a multi-tude of aspects, sexual, social, religious, but it can be reduced to a change in the quality of being from a state of infantile filthiness to a state of clean maturity. The ordeals undergone by the novices, of which the most conspicuous is circum-cision, are symbolic, as we have seen, of the initiatory death. But what is in question is always a death to something which has to be surpassed. The novice dies to be transformed or transmuted, and attain to a higher quality of existence. This is death to the indistinct and amorphous state of childhood (implicit in the meaning of *mudyi*), in order to be reborn into masculinity and personality.

BIBLIOGRAPHY

ARENSBERG, C. M. 1938. *The Irish Countryman*. Harvard University Press.

—— & KIMBALL, S. T. 1940. *Family and Community in Ireland*. Harvard University Press.

BATESON, G. 1936. *Naven*. Cambridge University Press.

BOTT, E. 1957. *Family and Social Network*. London: Tavistock.

BUSIA, K. A. 1951. *The Position of the Chief in the Modern Political System of Ashanti*. Oxford University Press for International African Institute.

CARGILL THOMPSON, W. D. J. 1956. Unpublished dissertation: 'The Two Regiments'. King's College, Cambridge.

COLSON, E. 1962. *The Plateau Tonga of Northern Rhodesia: Social and Religious Studies*. Manchester University Press for the Rhodes-Livingstone Institute.

COSER, L. 1956. *The Functions of Social Conflict*. Routledge and Kegan Paul.

COULANGES, FUSTEL DE. 1864. *La Cité Antique*. Paris: Hachette. Translated, 1956, *The Ancient City*. New York: Doubleday Anchor.

DENNIS, N., HENRIQUES, F., & SLAUGHTER, C. 1956. *Coal is our Life*. Eyre and Spottiswoode.

DURKHEIM, E. 1893. *De la division du travail social*. Paris: Alcan. Translated by G. Simpson: *The Division of Labour in Society*. Glencoe, Illinois: The Free Press, 1933.

—— 1913. *Les formes elementaires de la vie religieuse*. Paris: Alcan. Translated by G. Simpson: *Elementary Forms of Religious Life*. Allen and Unwin, 1915.

EISENSTADT, S. 1956. *From Generation to Generation*. Glencoe, Illinois: The Free Press.

EVANS-PRITCHARD, E. E. 1933. 'The Intellectualist (English) Interpretation of Magic', *Bulletin of the Faculty of Arts of Cairo University*. Vol. I, Part II.

EVANS-PRITCHARD, E. E. 1937. *Witchcraft, Oracles and Magic among the Azande*. Oxford: Clarendon Press.

—— 1948. *The Divine Kingship of the Shilluk of the Anglo-Egyptian Sudan*. Cambridge University Press.

—— 1956. *Nuer Religion*. Oxford: Clarendon Press.

FIRTH, R. 1955. *The Fate of the Soul*. Cambridge University Press.

FORDE, D. 1937. 'Land and Labour in a Cross River Village, S. Nigeria', *Geographical Journal*, xc, 1.

—— 1938. 'Fission and Accretion in the Patrilineal Clans of a Semi-Bantu Community in Southern Nigeria', *J.R.A.I.*, lxviii, pp. 311–38.

—— 1941. *Marriage and the Family among the Yakö in South-Eastern Nigeria*. Lund Humphries. 2nd edition, International African Institute, 1955.

—— 1946. *The Native Economies of Nigeria*. Vol. 1 of *The Economics of a Tropical Dependency*, ed. Margery Perham. Faber & Faber.

—— 1949. 'Integrative Aspects of Yakö First Fruits Rituals', *J.R.A.I.*, lxxix, pp. 1–10.

—— 1950. 'Ward Organisation among the Yakö', *Africa*, xx, pp. 267–89.

—— 1954. *African Worlds: Studies in the Cosmological Ideas and Social Values of African Peoples*. Oxford University Press for the International African Institute.

—— 1957. *The Context of Belief: a consideration of fetishism among the Yakö*. Liverpool University Press.

—— 1958. 'Spirits, Witches and Sorcerers in the Supernatural Economy of the Yakö', *J.R.A.I.*, lxxxviii, 2, pp. 165–78.

—— 1961. 'The Governmental Roles of Associations among the Yakö', *Africa*, xxxi, pp. 309–23.

FORTES, MEYER. 1945. *The Dynamics of Clanship among the Tallensi*. Oxford University Press for the International African Institute.

—— 1949a. *The Web of Kinship among the Tallensi*. Oxford University Press for the International African Institute.

FORTES, MEYER (Ed.). 1949b. *Essays presented to A. R. Radcliffe-Brown*. Oxford, Clarendon Press.

—— 1959. *Oedipus and Job in West African Religion*. Cambridge University Press.

—— 1961. 'Pietas in Ancestor Worship', *J.R.A.I.*, xci, 2.

—— & EVANS-PRITCHARD, E. E. (Eds.). 1940. *African Political Systems*. Oxford University Press for the International African Institute.

FRANKENBERG, R. J. 1957. *Village on the Border*. Cohen and West.

FRANKFORT, HENRI. 1948. *Kingship and the Gods*. University of Chicago Press.

FÜRER-HAIMENDORF. 1953. 'The After-Life in Indian Tribal Belief', *J.R.A.I.*, lxxxiii.

GENNEP, ARNOLD VAN. 1909. *Rites de Passage*, Paris: Emile Nourry. Translated by Monika B. Vizedom and Gabrielle L. Caffee as *The Rites of Passage*, Routledge and Kegan Paul, 1960, with an introduction by S. T. Kimball.

GEORGES, KARL, E. & H. 1959. *Ausführliches Lateinisch-Deutsches Handwörterbuch*. 10th edition. Basel.

GLUCKMAN, M. 1936. 'The Realm of the Supernatural among the South-Eastern Bantu.' Unpublished D.Phil. thesis. Copies at the Bodleian Library and the Institute of Social Anthropology, Oxford; Department of Social Anthropology at the Universities of Manchester and of the Witwatersrand.

—— 1937. 'Mortuary Customs and the Belief in Survival after Death among the South-Eastern Bantu', *Bantu Studies*, xi.

—— 1954. *Rituals of Rebellion in South-east Africa* (the Frazer Lecture, 1952). Manchester University Press. Republished in Gluckman (1963).

—— 1955a. *The Judicial Process among the Barotse of Northern Rhodesia*. Manchester University Press for the Rhodes-Livingstone Institute.

—— 1955b. *Custom and Conflict in Africa*. Blackwell.

GLUCKMAN, M. 1961 .'African Jurisprudence', *The Advancement of Science*, No. 74 (Nov.).

—— 1963. *Order and Rebellion in African Tribal Society*. Cohen and West.

——, MITCHELL, J. C., & BARNES, J. A. 1949. 'The Village Headman in British Central Africa', *Africa*, xix, pp. 100 f. Republished in Gluckman (1963).

GOFFMAN, ERVING. 1959. *The Presentation of Self in Everyday Life*. New York: Doubleday Anchor.

GOODY, J. (Ed.). 1958. *Domestic Groups Cambridge Papers in Social Anthropology*, No. 1. Cambridge University Press.

—— 'Religion and Ritual: the Definitional Problem', *British Journal of Sociology*, xii, 2 (June).

HARRIS, R: Unpublished M.A. thesis at the University College, London.

HOERNLÉ, A. W. 1925. 'The Importance of the Sib in the Marriage Ceremonies of the South-eastern Bantu', *South African Journal of Science*, xxii, pp. 481 f.

HUBERT, H., & MAUSS, M. 1899. 'Essai sur la nature et fonction sociale du sacrifice', *Année Sociologique*, ii, pp. 29–138. Reprinted in Hubert and Mauss: *Mélanges d'histoire des religions*, Paris: Librairie Felix Alcan, 1929.

HUGHES, EVERETT C. 1958. *Men and their Work*. Glencoe, Illinois: The Free Press.

JUNOD, H. P. 1898. *Les Ba-Ronga*. Neuchatel: Paul Attinger.

—— 1913. *The Life of a South African Tribe*. London: Macmillan (second edition 1927).

—— n.d. *circa* 1934. *Henri A. Junod: Missionnaire et Savant*, Lausanne: Mission Suissse dans l'Afrique du Sud.

KANTOROWICZ, ERNST H. 1957. *The King's Two Bodies*. Princeton University Press.

LAGRANGE, PÈRE. 1905. *Etudes sur les religions semitiques*. Paris.

LINTON, RALPH. 1936. *The Study of Man*. New York: Appleton-Century Co.

LLOYD WARNER, W. 1937. *A Black Civilization*. New York: Harper.

MARWICK, M. G. 1952. 'The Social Context of Cewa Witch Beliefs', *Africa*, xxi.

MIDDLETON, J. F. 1960. *Lugbara Religion*. Oxford University Press for International African Institute.

NADEL, S. F. 1957. *The Theory of Social Structure*. Cohen and West.

PARSONS, TALCOTT. 1937. *The Structure of Social Action*. Glencoe, Illinois: The Free Press.

—— 1951. *The Social System*. Glencoe, Illinois: The Free Press.

POLLOCK, SIR FREDERICK, & MAITLAND, F. W. 1898. *History of English Law before the Time of Edward I*. Cambridge University Press.

RADCLIFFE-BROWN, A. R. 1922. *The Andaman Islanders*. Cambridge University Press.

—— & FORDE, D. (Eds.). 1950. *African Systems of Kinship and Marriage*. Oxford University Press for the International African Institute.

RATTRAY, R. S. 1927. *Religion and Art in Ashanti*. Oxford: Clarendon Press.

—— 1929. *Ashanti Law and Constitution*. Oxford: Clarendon Press.

REDFIELD, ROBERT. 1953. *The Primitive World and its Transformations*. Cornell University Press.

RICHARDS, A. I. 1939. *Land, Labour and Diet in Northern Rhodesia*. Oxford University Press for the International African Institute.

—— 1956. *Chisungu*. Faber & Faber.

—— 1960. 'Social Mechanisms for the Transfer of Political Rights in Some African Tribes', *J.R.A.I.*, xc, 2.

SCHAPERA, I. 1955. 'The Sin of Cain', *J.R.A.I.*, lxxxv.

SIMMEL, G. 1955. *Conflict and the Web of Group Affiliations*. Translated from the German by K. Wolff and R. Bendix. Glencoe, Illinois: The Free Press.

SOUTHALL, A. W. 1959. 'An Operational Theory of Role', *Human Relations*, xii, 1.

SRINIVAS, M. N. 1952. *Religion and Society among the Coorgs.* Oxford: Clarendon Press.

SUNDKLER, B. 1948. *Bantu Prophets in South Africa.* Lutterworth. 2nd edition 1961. Oxford University Press for the International African Institute.

TALMON, YONINA. 1959a. 'Social Structure and Family Size', *Human Relations*, xii.

—— 1959b. 'Sex-role Differentiation in an Equalitarian Society': paper presented to the third International Sociological Association Congress at Stresa.

TER HAAR, B. 1948. *Adat Law in Indonesia*, edited in translation by E. A. Hoebel and A. A. Schiller. New York: Institute of Pacific Relations.

TURNER, V. W. 1957. *Schism and Continuity in an African Society.* Manchester University Press for Rhodes–Livingstone Institute.

—— 1961a. 'Ritual Symbolism, Morality and Social Structure among the Ndembu', *Rhodes–Livingstone Journal*, No. 30. Manchester University Press.

—— 1961b. *Ndembu Divination: its Symbolism and Techniques*, Rhodes–Livingstone Papers, No. 31. Manchester University Press.

—— 1962. *Chihamba, the White Spirit*, Rhodes–Livingstone Papers, No. 33. Manchester University Press.

WEBER, MAX. 1930. *The Protestant Ethic and the Spirit of Capitalism.* Allen and Unwin.

—— 1947. *Theory of Social and Economic Organization.* Hodge & Co., London.

WHITE, C. M. N. 1948. 'Notes on Some Metaphysical Concepts of the Balovale Tribes', *African Studies*, vii.

—— 1953. 'Notes on the Circumcision Rites of the Balovale Tribes', *African Studies*, xii, 2.

—— 1961. *Elements in Luvale Beliefs and Rituals*, Rhodes–Livingstone Institute Paper 33. Manchester University Press.

WHYTE, W. H. 1956. *The Organization Man.* New York: Simon and Schuster.

Wilson, M. 1957. *Rituals of Kinship among the Nyakyusa*. Oxford University Press for the International African Institute.

—— 1959a. *Communal Rituals among the Nyakyusa*. Oxford University Press for the International African Institute.

—— 1959b. *Divine Kingship and 'the Breath of Men'*. Cambridge University Press.

INDEX

abdication: Ashanti law of, 60

accountability, 73; office as sacred trust, 78; of tenant and owner, 81

adat law, 30

adolescence, 16, 56

admission: payments to associations, 94, 96, 98 f., 110 f.; power emphasis in, 119; son's interest in, 112

age-set, 104, 109 f.

aggregation, 35

agreement: public approval, 80

agricultural ritual: Gluckman on, 15; and land transfer, 179 f.; and social relations, 30; among Swazi, 31; Tallensi cycle of, 74

ambiguity of role, 41

America, organization man in, 48

anarchy, 70

ancestor spirits: causing menstrual trouble, 151; control fertility, 140; demand inheritance of name, 146; in hunting ritual, 132; in initiation rites, 170; *muyombu* tree shrine, 138; names of circumcised, 167; (*mukishi*), not in newborn, 131-2; petitioned before rituals, 143; petitioned with white beer, 162; related to whiteness, 142-3

ancestor-veneration: associated trees, 145

ancestral land, transfer of, 79

Andaman Islanders, 38, 50

anointing: with white clay, 143

anthropology, 4, 10, 14, 50, 53 f.

anxiety, 31 f., 37

Arabs, 6n.4

Arensberg, C. M., 36, 47

arrow: symbol of masculinity, 133-134, 165

ase (*see* fetish)

Ashanti, 59-60, 69, 85

association (*see also* Yakö): and mortuary rites, 90, 97, 113, 122

authority (*see also* Fortes, multiplex relationships, Yakö): checks on, 74; investment of legal, 35; and office, 59; ritual support of, 86; of Tallensi chiefship, 65; in Zulu first-fruits rites, 31

avoidance (*see also* taboos), 27-8, 33

Barotse, 27, 34, 59

Bateson, G., 40n.1, 42n.2

Bedouin, 41

beer, 'white maize', used for petitioning ancestors, 162; kaffircorn and maize—as white symbols, 140

Bemba, 74

'black': blood, 148; colour of lust, 135

'blocked exegesis', results from norm-conflict, 164

blood: circumcision—lethal power, 162; kinds of and significance for Ndembu, 147-54; stemming of after circumcision, 168

Bott, E., 36

bow (*see mudyi* tree)

Brahmans, 7

bride-price, 63

brother, older: as father's deputy, 157

burial: of foetus, 131; of hunters, 132; of placenta and umbilical cord, 132

Burier of the Matrikin, 91

cassava mush: symbol of semen, 148

castration (*see* circumcision)

ceremonial (*see also* Gluckman: definition; multiplex relationships): in Britain, 48; contrasted with ritual, 21, 30; in family economic enterprise,